The Writing Skill Builder for College Freshmen

Revised Edition

By Joy F. Beckford

Palm Beach State College

cognella™
San Diego, CA

First published in the United States of America in 2010 by Cognella, a division of University Readers, Inc.

14 13 12 11 10   1 2 3 4 5

Printed in the United States of America

ISBN: 978-1609279-96-7

www.cognella.com 800.200.3908

Acknowledgments

SINCEREST GRATITUDE IS extended to all students who have suggested (from semester to semester) that I write this workbook to help future freshmen. I must also thank those whose writings have reflected marked improvement as they applied skills reviewed semester after semester, which proves that "Practice makes perfect." Be assured that such positive attitude toward learning has continuously reinforced my faith in expecting the best from all my students in the teacher-student learning process.

Many thanks are extended to my co-workers—professors, who have shared their concerns about improving students' writing. To those writers whose insightful passages I have adapted and modified to accommodate the exercises, my gratitude is extended, too. In addition, I would not be forgiven if I did not acknowledge my beautiful daughter Tamica as well as my sister Beverley whose questioning, prodding, and encouragement further motivated me to complete this workbook, and I would be remiss to omit Carolyn Carter, the editors, the publisher, and all the other University Readers' team members who have directly contributed toward the success of this text.

About the Author

JOY F. BECKFORD is an English teacher who writes from years of experience. She is a Sigma Tau Delta scholar with a Master's degree in English from State University of New York College at Brockport. Her array of knowledge, regarding students' learning, spans from years of teaching in Caribbean and American classrooms, and her forte is to help all students become more comfortable with writing, as they develop mastery of the writing skills. Her passion and love for English are reflected in another workbook entitled Grade Nine Achievement Tests in English which challenges high school students to prepare for college-level work. She has taught at all levels including Monroe Community College in New York and now teaches at Palm Beach State College in Florida.

Contents

Contents

Preface

TO STUDENTS:

WELCOME TO THE arena of higher learning and advanced writing. Perhaps you may be unaware that to obtain a degree, certain liberal arts' courses are mandatory whether you are at a four-year university or a two-year community college, and Composition is one of them. Either way, nearly all courses mandate some form of academic writing. Stephen King suggests that to write well, one "must do two things above all others: read a lot and write a lot." In addition, mechanics such as comma splices, parallelism, appropriate use of commas, fragments, linking ideas with transitions, subject-verb agreement, and other writing skills must be applied during the writing process. Sometimes, even those who have learned these skills well in elementary and high school often find themselves struggling to write well, especially under pressure of fulfilling course assignments. Academic writing, therefore, becomes even more tedious for those who have struggled just to pass that English course in high school, but do not worry, for all who have gone through college have had to face this hurdle: writing well. That is why this workbook is prepared with simple exercises (as close as possible to students' phrasings) to provide extensive focus on your particular weaknesses, not only to bridge the gap between bad and good writing but also to help all users achieve As, Bs, and Cs, instead of Ds and Fs.

Reading widely is definitely essential to intellectual or academic writing, so I am encouraging you to start reading even a secular magazine or the local newspaper daily if you are not already an avid reader. Furthermore, subconsciously, emulating good writing styles do help immensely in learning the art of writing, as ardent writers reinforce mechanics of the standard forms (of any language), which if not properly gleaned, many—even those with degrees—may or may not be able to identify, for example, even faulty comma usage (or lack thereof). A wrong use or non-use (of a comma), sometimes creates misinterpretation of writers' viewpoints. For instance, look closely at the same sentence meanings with just comma placements: 1. "Woman, without her man, is nothing." 2. "Woman, without her, man is nothing." King further reiterates in "On Writing" that extensive reading enables one to differentiate between good and bad writing, since "Every [piece of work] … has its own lesson or lessons, and quite often the bad books [or essays] have more to teach than the good ones."

Since writing is an integral part of nearly all college courses, this workbook is particularly written to help you—in-coming students— especially those who have left school awhile and are now thrust into higher levels of academic writing. These exercises are also very useful to repeating students who have failed classes because of poor writing skills. In this edition, I have only focused on a few of the weakest areas that most often abound in students' writings, those that create frustration for students (when they receive graded papers) and for the professors (who have to grade the writing) from semester to semester. In fact, I am challenging those who have an aptitude for writing to challenge your own skills with these exercises.

Answer keys (with possible revisions) are included after "writing errors to avoid." Be honest, and try not to check the answers before completing each exercise, and remember that, except for correct sentences, the revisions can be done in different ways as long as original concepts are maintained. It is important to use your own perspective (called voice) in these responses. Further practice can be gleaned from whatever handbook your professor recommends or from any good English Grammar text provided in all libraries, as studies reveal that adults learn better by teaching themselves. Note that the way we habitually speak in our local environments, especially in non-educational settings, in our every-day conversations with those with whom we are familiar, sometimes hampers recognition of what is standard from non-standard English, and this usually becomes a major deterrent in writing well. For example, while it is all right (not alright) to say "OK, you guys; me and my kids; I be hanging out with my friends," and a myriad of clichés in informal setting, speech, and writing, these terms are unacceptable in formal speaking and writing, for example, at a job interview or in an application that requires some writing.

Remember that in most college writing, language must be formal. Your professor will tell you when informality is needed in assignments, and even in these instances, usage should never be too "lax," unless it is direct speech. Be cognizant also that nearly all colleges have learning centers where professional tutors are paid to help students write better papers—focusing on each individual's repetitive weaknesses.

Because this workbook is American-based, spellings and many phrasings are typically American, as in the well-known idiom: "When in Rome, do as the Romans do." This means that in an educational setting outside of America, where writing is necessary, use British spellings; in America, use American (for example: color, not colour; license for both noun and verb; traveled not travelled; practice, not practise; check, not cheque—payment for work). If unsure, use a dictionary. I am confident that this workbook, with many short passages and easy-to-do exercises (with simple explanations), will help you surmount, at least, the skills in the specific areas addressed. I know the challenge will be rewarding, as you develop understanding and grow into a better writer as well as a more knowledgeable speaker. I have also added a present tense verb bank to provide a variety of synonyms for "say" to augment argumentative and research writing as well as a list of informal words in the dictionary.

TO PROFESSORS:

My major mission as an educator is to touch the lives of as many students as possible by helping them to surmount much of the frustration that comes with understanding the art of writing well; therefore, I hope this workbook will be a helpful resource to lighten your task as you help your students to better overcome repetitive writing errors in the areas covered. I have also added, for your convenience, essay assignments linked to some of the exercises as well as a few short five to ten minutes warm-up exercises that may be done at the beginning of class.

One assumption, expressed by a number of my colleagues, is that students entering college should know the basic principles of writing, but unfortunately, this is a myth. Since many students have either forgotten the foundation rules of English or did not learn them well, it is advisable that weak skills are reviewed before assigning the exercises. This will strengthen even the best writers' skills as well as provide the opportunity for individuals to query confusing areas that some may be too intimidated to address openly, even during individual conferences. Together, as English teachers and educators, we can work as a team to help our students enjoy writing to achieve academic excellence.

For added practice, I recommend that these supplementary exercises be used along with those in the selected handbook. They may also be applied to group work and homework as well, especially for second language speakers. Students should also be encouraged to work individually on sections pertaining to their particular weaknesses, and extra credit could be awarded to those who show drastic improvement in writing after completing sections relevant to their weakness. I look forward to your comments and recommendations at beckforj@palmbeachstate.edu.

Clichés

Note: Your professor may decide to change directives given in any of the exercises in this workbook to accommodate writings skills for a particular class session or sessions.

AVOIDING CLICHÉD WRITING

LOOK AT THESE expressions: The rest is history; suck it up; he or she watches my back; my parents raised a stink when my brother came in drunk; we do not know what went down; we partied all night; the committee kicked off the tour/program; some of my family would throw me under the bus; T.J needs a wake up call; the thugs were in my grill; both friends were at each other's throat; my parents kicked me out of the house; O.J. found himself in hot water for allegedly killing his wife; go back to the drawing board. I could go and on, but now I am sure you "get my drift."

Are you guilty of using any of these or similar terminologies in formal writing, as in a research paper? Perhaps, the answer is yes. Has anyone ever told you that these expressions are unacceptable in standard speaking and writing? If not, now you are aware they must be avoided if not quoted, or used in dialog, or specifically used with quotation marks around the phrase (see "get my drift" above) to emphasize the specific point.

What exactly is a cliché? In *Oxford Advanced Learner's Dictionary*, it is explained as "a phrase or an idea that has been used so often that it no longer has much meaning and is not interesting." Why then do so many college students mistakenly use them for formal English? Perhaps, it is the fact that such usages give language a special flare and rhythm to the ear and make oral speaking more relatable to close friends and family members because of its flourish; nonetheless, they are informal thus are inappropriate in any formal document as well as in most college essays. In creative writing, plays, and dialect, however, they are acceptable, as they reflect the cultural diversity of spoken lingua franca of a people. For example, if I say, "My mother's death hit me like a ton of bricks, as she seemed hale and hearty," would audiences who have never heard these terms understand what I mean? For better clarity and freshness of thought, a possible revision could be "I was extremely shocked at my mother's untimely death, as she seemed very "strong and healthy." In *Elements of Language*, the writers better explain why writing formally is so challenging for many students, yet this inadequacy cannot be ignored:

> In the U.S., standard English is usually more a matter of writing than of speech. It is used for treating important matters seriously, and it is especially appropriate for talking with or writing to people we don't know well. It is the language of public affairs and education, of television, of science and technology, and of business and government. [Therefore,] people are expected to use [formal usages] in most schools and business situations (Odell et al. 941).

Direction: Many of the sentences in exercises 1 to 5 have clichés. Follow the prompts in each section. Possible revisions are in answer keys at back, but sentences can be revised in other ways, as long as your explanations do not change the implied ideas. Try to complete each exercise before checking the key.

Exercise 1 Circle all clichés, then, explain clearly in standard English what each means. Put a check beside those that need no revision.

1. Failing at something is not the end of the world; not persevering to overcome the hurdles is failure.

2. The basketball team pretty much pulled out all the stunts to win their opponents.

3. James threw a fit when his brother crashed his car.

4. America needs to become more competitive in the global economy to maintain its super-power status.

5. Fast-foods are so appetizing that many diners forget about weight and let themselves go.

6. Many young people as well as adults enjoy hanging out at the mall.

7. Tony got me pumped up with the news that I had won four free tickets to the basketball game where Michael Jordon and Shaq O'Neal would be playing.

8. Get off your high horse, and face the fact that not everyone is born with a gold spoon in the mouth.

9. Bullies never pick on those who challenge them, but mostly on timid introverts.

10. Keisha's husband knows what button to push to get her riled up.

Exercise 2 Reconstruct the sentences that have clichés into standard forms, or write "Correct" for those that need no revision.

1. The boys were into me and I into them.

2. What the proposal boils down to is the fact that the committee's decisions stand.

3. Religious controversies are inevitable, as there are those who will take the debate to a whole new level.

4. After sacrificing financially and emotionally for my siblings, their ingratitude is a slap in the face.

5. As the pastor addressed the congregation about forgiving those who have wronged us, something popped in my head.

6. Ridiculing or mimicking others always affects their self-esteem negatively.

7. When I am lonely and bored, to avoid depression, I like to hang out with my friends.

8. James and Suzan study for the mathematics examination, so they both pass with flying colors.

9. Robert Reich, a social class expert, says, "Social class is a very hot topic."

10. If there are better role models in the environments in which children grow, there will be less youthful dissidents in local communities, especially among the lower-income groups.

Exercise 3 Replace all clichés with standard English expressions, and put X beside sentences that need no change.

1. Sometimes, when students have such crazy schedules, they often cannot function well with the demanding course work.

2. "I am standing here like a piece of chop liver," says Dr. Phil.

3. A number of students purport that English skills are not shoved down their throats in high school which makes it very difficult to write well in college.

4. Unemployment forces parents to worry about putting food on the table.

5. Growing up in poverty has its advantage, as not having much often creates thrifty and prudent individuals.

6. Those who encounter near-death experience often believe they get a new lease on life.

7. Procrastination is a twenty-four seven habit for lazy people.

8. When Martha told Jimmy she was pregnant, he flipped out.

9. Immediately after hurricane Katrina, a number of residents, who lived in New Orleans all their lives, were completely displaced.

10. Since Deena was going solo, Martha asked her for a ride to the arena.

Exercise 4 Write NV for "Needs Revision" at the end of non-standard sentences. Underline and revise, if needed. Draw an oblique line through the number that represents any sentence that needs no revision.

1. America needs to jump on the bandwagon to clean up the environment to control global warming and to be more competitive with China in education and productivity.

2. Having a balanced diet, getting adequate sleep, and doing regular exercise promote good health.

3. "Foolish" is often a stigma assigned to young people, but many prove that they have a good head on their shoulder.

4. Most addicts do not want help until they hit rock bottom.

5. The exercise challenge is so difficult that the obese participants quit cold turkey.

6. If these negative individuals refuse to change, we should kick them to the curb.

7. It is stereotypically believed that many Asian-Americans chose in vitro fertilization to have boys over girls.

8. The former Illinois Governor Blagovojevich is very mad at Congress who impeached him for his alleged effort to sell President Obama's senate seat.

9. Sarah Palin, former governor of Alaska, has a grouse against the media for treating her unfairly because she is a woman.

10. When the President of the United States vetoes a bill, he disagrees with the proposal(s).

Exercise 5 Work with a group or a partner to change all clichés or idiomatic adages below to formal phrasings, then create a realistic narrative (about two pages) in half an hour (your professor might change time allotted). Try to incorporate, at least, eight of the standard changes, and be sure to write interestingly as well as realistically.

1. keep a person down

2. having thick and thin skin

3. blow my mind

4. dancing one's socks off

5. get a handle on the problem

6. to have a lot going on

7. to have cool family or friends

8. to be up in someone's grill

9. to have a problem with no end in sight

10. drawing a blank when asked a question

NOTES

Comma Splices

THE CONFUSING COMMA SPLICE

PERHAPS, THE COMMA splice is a constant deterrent in your obtaining that A for an essay that has a number of repetitive commas between independent clauses with no transition after sentence 1. This tells the reader that the writer does not know where a sentence ends. However, correcting the error is easy, once the principle is understood. Look carefully at sentence 1; look at the comma between "States" and "his." That is a comma splice.

Incorrect

* Barack Obama believed he could be the next president of the United States, his opponent, John McCain, believed that was impossible for his sheer inexperience.

> The comma can stay there, but a transition is needed to connect the two independent clauses. A semicolon or period could be used, too, depending on the sentences. If the period (US) or full stop (BrE) is used, a capital letter must begin sentence 2 (e.g. his to His). Fixing the comma splice is as easy as that. Sometimes, however, adding a transition is more appropriate than adding a semicolon, especially if the ideas are not closely related (see handbook for appropriate semicolon usage, as quite a number of students abuse its use).

Carefully examine the possible revisions:

* Barack Obama believed he could be the next president of the United States, **though**
transition added
his opponent John McCain believed that was impossible for his sheer inexperience.

* Barack Obama believed he could be the next president of the United States; his op-
semicolon added
ponent, John McCain believed that was impossible for his sheer inexperience.

* Barack Obama believed he could be the next president of the United States. His op-

period and **capital letter added**

ponent, John McCain, believed that was impossible for his sheer inexperience.

Whole-class exercise:

Now, try to rewrite the sentences below correctly before attempting Exercises 6 to 10.

a. Studies show that Blacks need more vitamin D than Caucasians, thus they need to get ten to fifteen minutes of natural sunlight daily, supplementary tablets are also recommended or an increase of green leafy vegetables.

b. The lexicon of English is constantly changing, a number of new slang and colloquial expressions are accepted as the standard, while some usages have either become outmoded, obsolete, or too antiquated for the each generation.

c. Health-conscious individuals prefer organic instead of gene-altered foods, some, however, do not care for either, as long as they have food.

d. Advertisements bait consumers into sporadic spending, those with bad credit often pay more for purchases.

Direction: Punctuations and minor capitalization changes have been made in Exercise 6 to Exercise 10 to accommodate practice in recognizing comma splice errors. Read the prompts carefully.

Exercise 6 Review the paragraph below for comma splices and put CS where they occur. Afterwards, discuss your views in an essay regarding human cloning. Give the essay a suitable title. Your professor will determine the length.

For the past five years, the prospect of human cloning has been the subject of considerable public attention and sharp moral debate, both in the United States and around the world, since the announcement in February 1997 of the first successful cloning of a mammal (Dolly the sheep), several other species of mammals have been cloned. Although a cloned human child has yet to be born, and although the animal experiments have had low rates of success, the production of functioning mammalian cloned offspring suggests that the eventual cloning of humans must be considered a serious possibility.

In November 2001, American researchers claimed to have produced the first human embryos, though they reportedly reached only a six-cell stage before they stopped dividing and died, in addition, several fertility specialists, both here and abroad, have announced their intention to clone human beings. The United States Congress has twice taken up the matter, in 1998 and again in 2001-2002, with the House of Representatives in July 2001 passing strict ban on all human cloning, including the production of cloned human embryos, as of this writing, several cloning-related bills are under consideration in the Senate. Many other nations have banned human cloning, and the United States is considering an international convention on the subject.

—Dorothy U. Seyler, "Bioethics: A Brave New World"

Exercise 7 Rewrite the paragraph below without the comma splice errors, then emulate the style in an argumentative essay (your professor will decide when this essay is due and the length). Be sure to select an interesting title, and follow the advice given in the reading below.

Sometimes when we argue, it's easy to get carried away. Remember that your goal is to persuade and perhaps change your readers, not alienate them, instead of laying on insults or sarcasm, present your ideas in a moderate let-us-reason-together spirit. Such a tone will persuade your readers that you are sincere in your attempts to argue as truthfully and fairly as possible, if your readers do not respect you as a reasonable person, they certainly won't be swayed to your side of an issue. Don't preach or pontificate either; no one likes—or respects—a writer with a superior attitude, write in your natural "voice"; don't adopt a pseudo-intellectual tone. In short, to argue effectively, you should sound logical, sincere, and informed.

—Jean Wyrick, "Argumentation"

Exercise 8 After underlining the places where the comma splices occur, select a topic that reflects a certain period in history, as in the passage below, and let the reader see the changes in a two-page essay (single-spaced if written by hand; double-spaced if typed).

The Renaissance was a testing time for beliefs that had been held, sometimes very feebly, for many centuries. It was also a period when new ideas and forces were beginning to come into play. Hence the Renaissance was both modern and medieval—as is, for that matter, the "modern" age, which exhibits some emotional attitudes and beliefs that go back to medieval, ancient, even prehistoric times, the Renaissance material base was a late medieval heritage—urban populations, a money economy, and the beginning of a capitalist enterprise, with small but thriving cities to foster and disseminate culture. These socio-economic factors, so essential to the whole modern era, were not originated by or in the Renaissance. In fact, to some extent they were temporarily impaired during the fourteenth and fifteenth centuries by a drastic decline in population following the Black Death and by a contraction of industry and commerce in Italy and portions of northern Europe, accompanied by severe financial crisis. If modern society is dependent on the prominence of a middle class—the origins of which can be traced to the late Middle Ages—the trend in the leading centers of Italian Renaissance civilization was retrogressive, between the thirteenth and the late fifteenth centuries[,] the urban middle class in Italy—the most advanced region of European civilization—shrank in numbers and influence as commercial oligarchies gained ascendancy. Italian society was more aristocratic in tone at the end of the Renaissance than at the beginning, and in Europe as a whole the democratic tendencies implicit in the growth of self-governing towns during the late Middle Ages—in France, the Netherlands, and Germany as well as Italy—had been largely suppressed, it is true that some important changes in interests and activities pointed in a modern direction, notably increased travel, the introduction of printed books, and fumbling but essential efforts to unlock the secrets of nature. But it is [also] true that other equally important aspects of Renaissance society and culture were still oriented towards the past.

—Phillip Lee Ralph, "The Renaissance—Sunrise or Sunset"

Exercise 9 After correcting the comma splices in the excerpt below, dispute a fact in one paragraph as the writers below have done. Be sure to avoid comma splices and write clearly.

Surveys on sexual habits are notorious for inaccurate reporting: Invariably the number of times that women in the U.S. report that they engage in sexual intercourse with a man in the last week, or month, or year is much lower than the reports that men give of sexual intercourse with a woman during that time, the figures are so different that it would be impossible for both groups to be answering accurately. Generally, questionnaires and surveys are problematic, because questions need to be formulated without bias, even then, the interviewer has to rely on the respondent answering truthfully.

—Richard L Epstein and Carolyn Kernberger, "Generalization"

Exercise 10 Read this excerpt from Thomas Jefferson's "The Declaration of Independence," then correct any comma splices that exist in the draft. After you have completed this assignment, borrow the title, then write an introductory paragraph with a clear thesis to show that you understand exactly what Jefferson means. Your professor will decide whether it should be expanded into an essay to be shared with the class, what length, and the date it is due.

When in the course of human events, it becomes necessary for one people to dissolve the political bands which have connected them with another, and to assume among the powers of the earth, the separate and equal station to which the Laws of Nature and of Nature's God entitle them, a decent respect to the opinions of [hu]mankind requires that they should declare the causes which impel them to the separation.

We hold these truths to be self-evident, that all men [human beings] are created equal, that they are endowed by their Creator with certain inalienable rights, that among these are life, liberty, and the pursuit of happiness. That to secure these rights, governments are instituted among men/[women], deriving their just powers from the consent of the governed. That whenever any form of government becomes destructive of these ends, it is the right of the people to alter or to abolish it, and to institute new governments laying its foundation on such principles and organizing its power in such forms, as to them shall seem most likely to effect their safety and happiness. Prudence, indeed, will dictate that governments long established should not be changed for light or transient causes; and accordingly all experience hath shown that [hu]mankind are more disposed to suffer, while evils are sufferable, than to right themselves by abolishing the forms to which they are accustomed. But when a long train of abuses and usurpation, pursuing variably the same object, evinces a design to reduce them under absolute despotism, it is their right, it is their duty, to throw off such government, and to provide new guards for their future security. Such has been the patient suffering of these Colonies; and such is now the necessity which constrains them to alter their former systems of government.

—qtd. in Shrodes et al., *The Conscious Reader*

NOTES

Fragments

GETTING RID OF FRAGMENTS

To learn how to correct a fragment (subordinate clause), it is important to learn how to recognize it, and the simplest method that I can share with those who are unable to recognize it when writing or reading (apart from the linguistic testing approach) is to use the analogy of a broken leg depending on the other for support. This indicates that a fragment does not make sense by itself as reflected in the examples shown below borrowed directly from students' writings:

—For example, coming out with a good thesis, a strong topic sentence to capture, the audience and making an outline

* What did the writer discuss before? To what do the examples refer?

—Made sure we had a good dinner and our homework was done

* Who is doing the action here?

—The one person I can count on who would do anything for me

* Who is that person on whom the writer can depend?

Are you confused? Note that all three writers leave the audience as confused as you, as readers are now left to decipher and fill in possible meanings.

An easy method to fix fragments is to link them to the main clause (independent sentence) by adding a comma, as you would do after an introductory clause, or restructure the whole sentence by combining ideas and details, or make a new sentence with the fragment. Whichever you choose, ask yourself if the phrasing makes sense when read aloud. Perhaps the above fragments could be revised thus:

—In writing an essay, a clear thesis or topic sentence and an outline will capture the audience's interest.

—Mother made sure we had a [healthy] dinner and our homework done.

—My father is the only person on whom I can depend.

Are you confused with these revisions, or are the ideas clearer? As a rule, a sentence, called an independent clause, must have a subject and a verb which can stand alone, even without any additional explanation—extended predicate (e.g. <u>Bionce Kknoles</u>

Subject

<u>and Josh Broban</u> **sing melodiously and are awarded medals of honor for their**

Subject   Verb   Verb   Extended predicate

contribution to the music industry). Note two subjects joined by and take plural verb "are awarded" and "sing."

Note: The **highlighted** words (called fragment or dependent clause) will not be understood without the underlined subject and verb. They work "hand in hand." Each needs the other to convey full meaning to the audience.

Directions: Punctuation changes have been made in Exercises 11 to 15, to accommodate further practice in recognizing fragments. Follow the directives in each section.

Exercise 11 Put an asterisk beside all fragmented sentences (which are replicas of students' errors). Reconstruct them where possible, then use one or two independent clauses in a one and a half page narrative about the strangest experience you have had. This may be timed in class. Your professor will decide how much time is needed for this assignment.

1. Reason being that I can take all that I have learned and apply it to real life.

2. Human cloning, a scientific phenomenon, has sparked controversial debates among scientists, moralists, and Christians, so much so that government has vetoed any possibility of creating a human being.

3. Is the fact that the economic recession affects even the wealthy.

4. The racial divide in America is narrowing, but there are still milestones to go to bridge the educational, economic, and political gap.

5. In the mean time, coping with the stress of going to college, being a full-time mother, and working full time.

6. Which is not to imply that developed countries are not plagued with social problems such as poverty and unemployment.

7. Being an independent person who makes conscientious decisions to ensure the success of her children.

Exercise 12 Read the short passage below, then, answer the questions which follow.

The coming of the first Americans took place long before the writing of history began. How then do archeologists piece together the story of their arrival? The major way is by studying ancient **artifacts**—objects made by human beings. By examining such things as stone arrowheads, bone tools, or pieces of fur clothing. Archeologists can make reasonable guesses about how early peoples may have lived.

To locate artifacts, archeologists search for places where early people might have camped or hunted. Because thousands of years separate us from the first Americans. Many objects have been covered up or destroyed. Therefore, archeologists often must sift carefully through many layers of soil … [in a] … place … called an archeological dig.

—Devine et al., "The First Americans"

a. How many fragments are in the passage?
b. Underline them.
c. Rewrite the passage without the fragments, but do not add or delete any word. Use only appropriate punctuation and capitalization, if needed.
d. How much do know about your ancestry? Explain as clearly as possible avoiding fragments.

Exercise 13 In the passage below, adapted and modified to accommodate fragment practice, underline the areas where the fragments should be attached for cohesion. Do not add or delete any word. Only use appropriate punctuation and capitalization where necessary.

Most readers feel comfortable reading paragraphs that range between one hundred and two hundred words. Shorter paragraphs force too much stopping and starting, and longer ones strain readers' attention span. There are exceptions to this guideline, however. Paragraphs longer than two hundred words frequently appear in scholarly writing. Where they suggest seriousness and depth. Paragraphs shorter than one hundred words occur in newspaper because of narrow columns; in informal essays to quicken the pace, and in business writing and Web sites. Where readers routinely skim for main ideas.

In an essay, the first and last paragraphs will ordinarily be the conclusion. These special-purpose paragraphs are likely to be shorter than [those] in the body of the essay. Typically, the body paragraph will follow the essay's outline: on paragraph per point in longer essays. Some ideas require more development than others, however, so it is best to be flexible. If an idea stretches to a length unreasonable for a paragraph. You should divide the paragraph. Even if you have presented comparable points ... in single paragraphs.

—Diana Hacker, "Building Effective Paragraphs"

Exercise 14 (in-class exercise) Read this short paragraph to get the writer's full meaning, then revise it to eliminate any writing problems that exist. Now, borrow the title "A Creative Thinker" and compose an introductory paragraph with a clear thesis, about half page single-spaced. You can borrow one or two ideas from the reading as in-text citation, using Modern Language Association's (MLA) style of integrating sources.

A creative thinker must peek behind unquestioned ideas once in a while to keep from being close-minded. Doing this has led to some of humankind's most creative concepts the Declaration of Independence challenged the divine right of kings—the unquestioned belief that a king received his right to rule from God. Thomas Jefferson questioned this by stating that "All men are created equal." And that a king should rule. Not by God's authority, but by "the consent of the governed." What changes so few words have made in the world!

For centuries the dissection of the human body was forbidden. Until this unquestioned idea was challenged and the body dissected. People believed our emotions came from our our hearts (not our minds) and even thought a man's erection came from air in his lungs.

Unquestioned ideas are invisible to us because almost everyone takes them for granted, like eyesight or the ability to walk. When I mentioned Thomas Jefferson's famous phrases. Did you go one step further and ask if "all men are created equal" and [if] "consent of the governed" [is] also [being questioned] today? If challenging these ideas is upsetting. It's because our belief in them is deeply ingrained. [Buddha also reminds us to "Believe nothing because a belief is generally held"].

—M. Garrett Bauman, "Unquestioned Ideas"

Exercise 15 Here is an excerpt from Howard Gardner's essay "Leading Beyond the Nation-State." Read through the whole passage carefully to get the full sense of the ideas expressed before attempting to decipher where fragments exist. Now reread to connect the fragments, without changing the wording. Remember to follow the rules discussed on page 19. Do one paragraph at a time, unless your professor advises otherwise.

On rare occasions, individuals with neither vast armies nor vast congregations have succeeded in exerting influence well beyond national boundaries. Like the successful leaders of nations that we've already examined. They have done so because of the persuasiveness of their stories and the steadfastness with which they have reinforced those stories through their manner of living. In the twentieth century, three men stand out as exemplars in this category: Mohandas (Mahatma) Gandhi, Nelson Mandela, and Jean Monnet.

Perhaps the most well-known is Gandhi. Growing up in undistinguished surroundings in the late nineteenth-century colonial India, Gandhi spent time in England as a young man and then lived for twenty years in South Africa. There he was horrified by the mis-treatment by European colonizers of Indians and other "persons": he read widely in philosophy and religion; … he became involved in various protests. Returning to his native India at the start of the World War 1. Gandhi perfected methods of satyagraha—peaceful (non-violent) protest (or resistance). Alongside devoted countrymen, [he] led series of strikes and protest marches. Destined to throw into sharp relief the difference between the brutal English masters—who sought to hold power at any cost—and the non-belligerent Indians. These protests were choreographed to underscore the nobility of the native cause and the reasonableness with which Indians were striving to express their goals. Gandhi's overt message was: "We do not seek to make war or shed blood. We only want to be treated as fellow human beings. Once we have achieved the status of equals, we have no further claims."

In one sense, Gandhi's message could not have been simpler: It can be traced back to Christ and to the other religious leaders. Yet, it also clashed with an entrenched counter-story: that one can only attain an equal status vis-à-vis one's colonizers if—like the United States in the late eighteenth century or South America in the early nineteenth century—one is willing to go to war. Moreover, Gandhi did not only have a simple linguistic message; he also developed an integrated program of prayer, fasting, and facing one's opponent without weapons. Even willing to do so until death. His embodiment of the message could not have been more dramatic; it went well beyond verbal expression. To include a whole range of evocative formats, such as his squatting on the ground and operating a simple machine for spinning cloth.

Gandhi's story reverberated around the world. While annoying some (Churchill memorably disparaged him as that "Half-naked fakir"), it inspired many leaders and ordinary citizens—ranging from Martin Luther King Jr. in the American South in the early 1960s, to the students who rallied for greater democracy in Tiananmen Square in Beijing in 1989.

Like Gandhi, Nelson Mandela embodied a message that resonated on a level far beyond the borders of … South Africa. Indeed, of all the leaders in recent years, Mandela is widely considered one of the most impressive and influential. A lawyer by training, [he] became actively involved in resistance as part of the African National Congress. At first, he embraced non-violent resistance, but after a series of frustrating and degrading encounters, he joined a paramilitary group. Narrowly escaping death by combat or judicial sentence, [he] was imprisoned for twenty-seven years. Although such an experience would likely have demoralized, radicalized, or marginalized most other persons—especially since it occurred at middle age, often considered the apogee of an individual's person power—imprisonment seemed only to fortify Mandela.

Rather than seeking revenge against his opponents and jailers. Mandela called for reconciliation. He was convinced—and was able to convince others—that South Africa could not function as a society unless it could put its wrenching history behind it. Under the leadership of Nobel Peace Prize Winner Archbishop Desmond Tuto, Mandela convened a Commission of Truth and Reconciliation. The Gandhian idea behind this commission was that it would seek to establish what actually happened during the years of apartheid but would not attempt to sit in ultimate judgment. The truth having been established as well as it could be. Citizens of varying persuasions could come to terms with the past and commit their future energies to the buildup of a new and more fully representative society. A master of non-verbal as well as verbal forms, Mandela asked his one time jailer to sit in the front row during his presidential inaugural ceremony.

Mandela succeeded in changing the minds not only of millions of his otherwise diverse fellow citizens but equally of millions of observers around the world—few of whom would have predicted that South Africa [would] become a new nation without decades of bloodshed. Ideas like Commission on Truth and Reconciliation have traveled across national boundaries. The tipping points for Mandela's success entail both his exemplary behavior after his release from jail and the willingness of the entrenched South African leadership to negotiate with him—both examples reflecting [his] personal resonance, among other things.

A third figure of global importance worked largely behind the scenes: the French economist and diplomat Jean Monnet, born in 1888. When his comfortable life was shattered by the events of World War 1. Monnet—a careful and reflective student of history—pondered why it was necessary for European countries to go to war, as they had intermittently since the time of Charlemagne more than a thousand years before. He began to work towards the creation of institutions, that could bring about a united Europe. After the trauma of world War 1, the collapse of the League of Nations, the rise of fascism, and the unprecedented warfare of World War 11, a lesser person would have concluded that attempts to build a European community were futile. Monnet was a firm believer in his own oft-repeated slogan: "I regard every defeat (or challenge) as an opportunity. Amid the physical and psychological ruins of war-torn Europe. Monnet envisioned—and proceeded to sow—the seeds of a larger European polity.

—qtd. in Shrodes et al., *The Conscious Reader*

NOTES

Run-on or Fused Sentences

TAKING CARE OF RUN-ON OR FUSED SENTENCES

"RUN-ON," AS THE term denotes, means just that. This means independent sentences run together without periods (**period** is the American name for British **full stop**) in the appropriate places. Sometimes, this repetitive error comes from uncertainty and careless editing, but the omission of this punctuation makes the essay reading exhausting, confusing, and frustrating for the audience, especially when mixed with fragments and other mechanical errors. Imagine writing a long essay with periods only sporadically thrown in anywhere, as some students do. Imagine how difficult reading would become for the reading public, even for the educated, if the period rule is always broken. Do you think avid readers would still enjoy reading? For example, examine the struggle the writer of the sentence below gives readers to determine where each sentence ends.

* Social services in the United States will find adoptive families for abandoned or unwanted children this option is provided, especially for pregnant mothers who do not necessarily want an abortion, but they cannot afford to take care of a child, especially when abandoned by the child's father many of these parents are often teenagers who live in poverty in dysfunctional homes with unstable parents and a number of siblings.

Correct

Social services in the United States will find adoptive families for abandoned or unwanted children. This option is provided, especially for pregnant mothers who do not necessarily want an abortion, but they cannot afford to take care of a child, especially when neglected by the child's father. Many of these parents are often teenagers who live in poverty in dysfunctional homes with unstable parents and a number of siblings.

Direction (Whole–class exercise): You may work with a partner (with the professor's permission) to decipher where the periods should be in Exercise 16 before attempting Exercises 17–19 in which the period (full stop) rule may be broken. Follow the prompts in each section.

Exercise 16 If there are run-on or fused sentences in this set write "Yes," then punctuate the sentence(s) properly, if not write "No."

1. Women's Liberation Movement has empowered females, but the media still portray even the high achievers like Sarah Palin—Alaska's former governess; Michelle Obama—America's First black Lady, and Britain's Princess Diana—deceased wife of Prince Charles, as sex objects.

2. Nowadays, deoxyribonucleic acid' (DNA) tests provide proof to force negligent fathers, who deny the existence of their children, to accept financial responsibility if they refuse, the courts will enforce the law with either rigid fines or imprisonment.

3. Liberal arts program ensures that all college graduates are exposed to a wide array of knowledge this allows even those from the most impoverished socio-economic backgrounds and communities to become well-rounded and academically cultured.

4. An individual's childhood foundation will reflect itself in adulthood, though many facets of learned behaviors will change as the individual matures and analyzes his or her own experiences in contrast to that of others.

5. Learning is a continuous process, consciously and subconsciously many, however, seem to relish in the bliss of ignorance and denial about the value of education.

6. In the twenty-first century, a progressive country like America is forced to keep abreast of technological and scientific advances in order to compete with other growing economies.

7. Any good government must ensure adequate funding in the budget for advanced education this ensures that young people will have the opportunity to get advanced training to fill positions that demand academic knowledge and specialized skills.

Exercise 17 The paragraph below has a number of run-on sentences. Transcribe the whole filling in the missing periods to let the reading make sense.

It is scientifically proven that human beings are intrinsically social creatures and that socialization is pertinent to survival their finding is substantiated by numerous studies done by sociologists, anthropologists, archeologists, psychologists, and other schools of thought who further contend that one only has to observe nature itself to understand human interaction in correlation with the ecosystem it is evident that all creatures function within certain boundaries and within in-groups. Watch various birds in the air and on land, the schools of fish in the wide expanse of the oceans, seas, and rivers, the beasts of the fields, human beings at large in their ethnic groups versus in diverse gatherings, and even the variations of plants within certain climatic regions it seems that, except for the recluse, who consciously decides to exclude himself or herself from the human chain to live in vacuum, all other living things operate within the confines of their in-groups: family, friends, organizations, associations, and institutions this socialization process, therefore, becomes an integral part of human need not only to fulfill Abraham Maslov's hierarchy of needs—provision of food, shelter, and clothing—but also the need to feel part of a group, to develop self-actualization within the boundaries of those groups. While some prey on others, and the strong sometimes oppress the weak in organized societies and local communities, there is a universal understanding that every individual is innately gifted to serve a particular purpose in shaping the bond of humanity which is a clear indication that "No man [or woman] is an island."

Direction: Read the excerpt below taken from former President George W. Bush's "State of Our Union" address, after terrorists attacked the World Trade Center, the Twin towers, and other important buildings in America in 2001. Punctuation and capitalization changes have been made to accommodate this exercise.

Exercise 18 This exercise may have run-on sentences and should be completed in the maximum time of twenty minutes, unless advised otherwise. Rewrite the passage correctly, but do nothing, if there is no mistake.

I also want to speak to the Muslims throughout the world we respect your faith it is practiced freely by many Americans and by millions more in countries that America counts as friends its teachings are good and peaceful, and those who commit evil in the name of Allah blaspheme the name of Allah. The terrorists are traitors to their own faith, trying, in effect, to hijack Islam itself the enemy of America is not our many Muslim friends; it is not our many Arab friends. Our enemy is the radical network of terrorists and every government that supports them.

Our war on terror begins with Al Quaeda, but it does not end there it will not end until every terrorist group of the global reach has been found, stopped and defeated. Americans are asking, "Why do they hate us?"

—qtd. in Miller, "Writing to Inspire Others"

Exercise 19 (**in-class assignment—warm-up exercise**): In no more than five minutes, find where the run-on sentences occur). Only write the **two words** where the period should be.

High school students "have a gloomy view of the state of race relations in America today" according to a recent nationwide poll, students of all racial backgrounds brood about the subject. Another poll reveals that for the first time in this century, young white adults have less tolerant attitudes towards black Americans than those over thirty one reason is that "the under-30 generation is pathetically ignorant of recent American history." Too young to have experienced or watched the civil rights movement as it happened, these young people have no understanding of the past and present workings of racism in American society.

Educators justify teaching history because it gives us perspective on the present if there is one issue in the present to which authors should relate the history they tell the issue is racism. But as long as history textbooks make white racism invisible in the [twenty-first] century, neither they nor the students who use them will be able to analyze racism intelligently.

—James W. Lowen "The Invisibility of Racism in American History Textbooks"

Exercise 20 (**in-class activity**): Write a two-page expository essay—about four paragraphs—about your college experience, thus far. Be sure to revise the draft very carefully to eliminate all the run-on sentences, fragments, comma splices, and faulty grammar.

NOTES

Mixed Exercises

Directions: The following symbols may be used in the places where they are needed for cohesive reading in Exercise 21, but focus on the prompts in each:

CS = comma splice R-O = run-on sentence   vb. = subject-verb agreement

frag. = fragment   S = sentence without error   t = wrong tense

Exercise 21 There may be comma splices, run-on sentences, fragments, wrong word usage, faulty grammar, and unparallel structure in this passage. Underline the places where the errors occur, then put the appropriate symbols or correct words in place.

Standard English is a variety of language that is not limited to a particular place or ethnic group it is the one variety of English that is more widely used and accepted than any other in the United States. Because it is commonly understood. People from many different regions and cultures can communicate with one another clearly. In the U.S., standard English is more a matter of writing than of speech. It is used for treating important matters seriously, and it is especially appropriate for talking with or writing to people we don't know well. It is the language of public affairs and education, of publications and television, of science and technology, and of business and government. People are expect to use standard English in most schools ... businesses, and situations. It is also the variety of English recorded in dictionaries and grammar books.

Textbook presents and illustrate many of the rules and guidelines for using standard English. ... Nonstandard, [however,] does not mean wrong language, it means language that is inappropriate in situations where standard English is expected. Nobody needs to use standard English all the time, but everybody should be able to use it [when necessary].

—Lee Odell, Richard Vacca, and Renee Hobb's, "Standard English"

Exercise 22 Read this segment from "Blaming the Wrong Villain" regarding medical care in America in David Lindorff's discussion of "Marketplace Medicine" which has been modified to accommodate this exercise. As you read, try to identify fragments, comma splices, run-on sentences and subject-verb disagreement.

For years, as the costs of medical care have soared. Patients and taxpayers have taken in an iatrogenic view of the disease of medical cost inflation, rallying against doctors as the most visible symbols of the problem. While physicians as a group has grown fabulously rich since the institution of Medicare program for the elderly and disabled in 1965, they are hardly the major recipients of Health-care dollars. That distinction belongs to another sector of the industry: hospitals.

That Americans have tended to blame the doctor for their soaring medical bills should not elicit much surprise. Since most insurance plans have deductible, (the base amount a covered individual must pay in a year before any reimbursements is possible) and "co-pays" (an amount a patient must pay for any treatment), the cost of an average doctor's office visit is paid by the patient as a result, nearly everyone—even those who are basically healthy—have felt the sting of physician charges.

On the other hand, people doesn't get a bill from a hospital until they have had to spend some time in one. Then the bill's a whopper; the total amount [owed] is not only more than the initial deductible amount the patient must pay, but [it] is also into the major "medical portions" of the insurance plan which covers 100 percent of the bill. As a result, even if the patient has to pay a few hundred dollars for the initial deductible and the typical 20 percent of the first $1,000 or so, the remainder of the bill is paid by the insurance company, this naturally tends to salve most of the pain and make the hospital appear a much less vexing target.

—qtd. in Daniel J. Curran and Claire M. Renzetti

Exercise 23 Read the two paragraphs to grasp the writer's views, then, reread to correct all the errors that occur in the draft.

Humanity's interdependence seem to be cemented in our inward nature and is reinforced by the very way most societies are set up—either by some understood regulations set out by a tribe—like being circumcised a few days after birth, or those stipulated in documents like the American Constitution, sacred texts like the Bible, and the Qur'an we are so dependent on each other, in one way or another, that despite the social class in which we find ourselves, we still need each other. For example, as the chain needs every link for support and the large farmer harvesters for the crops, so the employers need workers to operate the conveyor lines in a factory as well as the machines, the unskilled needs the skilled; the ignorant needs the educated; the weak needs the strong; children need parents or vice versa.

It is with this understanding of the need for clanship and socialization that Will Durant not only proposed but also, with other modernist thinkers, "launched a movement" recorded in "the Congressional Record ... in 1945" to ensure mutual understanding in community camaraderie. A few of these proposals are cemented in The Declaration of Independence:

> [1] ... difference of race, color, and creed are natural ... diverse groups, institutions, and ideas are stimulating factors in the development of man/ [humanity].

> [2] ... to promote harmony in diversity is a responsible task of religion and statesmanship.

> [3] ... the realization of human interdependence and solidarity is the best guard of civilization.

Therefore, no one can deny that these universal truths do not uphold the pillars and stability of organized society. Institutions, organizations, social clubs, the workforce, the home.

Exercise 24 Subject-verb agreements may be faulty in these short paragraphs, modified to give you amply practice. Correct them, if there is any. Do not rewrite the whole paragraph, but the subject and verb only. Do not change the number of the subject, either. In other words, if it is plural or singular, keep it as is.

Sociology is the study of agreements and disagreements people have regarding their points of view. It is the study of harmony and conflict, order and disorder, persistence and change ... An agreement [can be defines as] ... a condition of being the same, and a disagreement is a condition of being different.

When you and I "make an agreement," we are simply creating a condition of being the same in some regard. When we agree to have lunch together, we creates a shared expectation about lunch: We both agree to the same thing. We would disagree if you expected that we have lunch together and I did not.

The agreements and disagreements that sociologists study, however, does not necessarily reflects the acts of people getting together and making agreements. Indeed, the greater part of sociology is devoted to agreements that has never been openly discussed and formed by the people who share them.

People can agree without knowing that they agree or even without knowing each other. This is an essential point. For example, even though we have never meet each other, you and I can agree that war is bad. Or we can disagree.

There is another aspect of social agreement that may not be immediately evident: You don't have to like an agreement in order to make it. When you were younger, for example, your parents may have set a time for you to be home. That curfew was an agreement, and you shares it with your parents even if you didn't like it. You may have had a different point of view on the necessity or justice of the curfew, and you may have argue with your parents about it. If you still accepted the expectation that you would get home on time, you and your parents had an [understood] agreement.

—Earl R. Babbie "The Nature of Agreement and Disagreements"

Exercise 25 Each of the sentences in this exercise may have a different error or may have none. If any is against standard writing protocol, rewrite it correctly.

1. Everybody has a right to their own viewpoints.

2. The reason why the three new employees lose the job is because of their lackadaisical attitude and repetitive tardiness.

3. Does not leave much hope for the future generation, especially children who are orphaned from a very early age.

4. A positive approach to life can be achieved through spirituality, there are skeptics, agnostics, and atheists who believe otherwise.

5. Joan protests, "Do you expect me to break the bank!"

6. Me and my family appreciates the kind gesture of financial and emotional support from the Red Cross and United Way, since the hurricane destroyed our house.

7. Volunteering at a nursing home is a good way to serve the community.

NOTES

Noun–Pronoun; Pronoun–Pronoun Parallels

NOUN–PRONOUN AND PRONOUN–PRONOUN PARALLELS WITH VERB AGREEMENT

TWO OF THE major weaknesses in students' writing are the misuse of Noun–Pronoun and Pronoun–pronoun parallels—called antecedents. Not only are they wrongly aligned, but also the wrong verbs are usually used in writing as well as in speaking. This repetitive misuse often creates imbalance in sentence structures, causes confusion for the readers—audience, and sometimes lends itself to contrasting ambiguous ideas.

Here are a few of the basic pronouns and nouns that give student writers much problem when used as subjects:

> each   someone   everyone   none   somebody   no one
> anybody   everybody   nobody   one   neither   either

* Be very careful also when sentences begin with the phrases below, as is extremely common in students' writing:

> when a person; when an individual; when a student.

* As a rule, all of the above are always equated with singular verbs, pronouns and nouns. Look at these two examples which seem correct:

is (correct)

1. **Each** of the workers **are** given $1,000 bonus at Christmas time.
   singular   plural (wrong verb—does not match subject **each**)

he or she (correct)

2. When **a person** breaks the law, <u>**they**</u> will be arrested if caught.

        singular   plural (wrong antecedent—not parallel to **person**)

One way to avoid these errors is to use plural nouns or pronouns. For instance, change each to all and a person to terms like dissidents, delinquents, people or any suitable term. Remember, in formal writing and speaking, it is very important not to use singular antecedents with plural nouns or pronouns and vice versa. Corresponding verbs must be used, too. Study other parallel usages below before attempting Exercises 26 to 30.

* Watch correct use of correlative conjunctions:

      —**Neither** is used with **nor**; **either** is used with **or**; **but also** is used with **not only**.

Parallelisms: —**Neither** the geologist **nor** the astronaut could decide whether or not the soil found on Mars can generate plant life.

               —**Either** Susan **or** Joan is eligible for the scholarship.

<u>Exception to the rule</u>: Look at the last subject to determine verb, when nor or or is used

      —Neither the girl nor her <u>**friends attend**</u> the party

      —Either the doctors or the <u>**nurse is**</u> negligent.

However, when "**of**" is used after **either** or **neither**, use singular verb (note example carefully: Neither **of** the graduates **is responsible** for cancellation of the party

* Look at "neither" as the subject, instead of "graduates. This rule is tricky, so be very careful to focus when the "of" is omitted or included in the sentence.

As **a rule**, both phrases "not only" and "but also" should be used together, as is. However, sometimes this rule can be broken by separating but and also, depending on the sentence context as shown in both examples below:

* **Not only** is water important to humans' survival **but also** to all living things in the eco-system as well.

Acceptable Broken Rule: Not only is water important to humans' survival, but it is also important to maintaining the eco-system.

NOTES

Tense Shifting

* Watch the parallelism in a sequence of verbs or ideas in a sentence, too

   Non-parallels may also appear in wrong **tense usage** called tense shifting: Look closely at the examples in these sentences:
   —The presidential nominees campaign and talked about opponents foibles (mixed tenses—(avoid shifts like this in the same sentence).
   Parallel tenses: campaign and talk or campaigned and talked

* Link coordinate ideas carefully:

   —Some animals **prefer preying** on other animals than **to eat** herbs.
   Correct Parallel Tense: **preying** and **eating**

   —The dance team **will compete** in the Olympics next year and **participate** in the local championship this year.
   Incorrect Parallel Tense: **will compete** and **will participate** not "participate" by itself.

   —After the hurricane destroyed the village, the frustrated home owners **rallied** in the streets, **collected** signatures from survivors, then **lead** a deputation to the White House to seek the president's intervention for financial assistance.
   Correct Parallel Tenses: After the hurricanes destroyed the village, the frustrated home owners **rallied ... collected ... led ...**

> Note the unity of the verb tense which could also be in other forms, for example, the present: destroy, rally, collect, lead; the future: will/shall destroy, will/shall rally, will/ shall lead. Note: Had the subject "home owners" been singular, the verbs would be destroys, rallies, collects, leads. Choice of tense is determined by time of action.

Since I am addressing verb tense, be reminded that the past participle verbs are never used by themselves. They need helpers to be used correctly. For example, the verbs in these three sentences are wrongly used:

1. The children gone to the store.
2. Sandy known for her creativity in sculptural designs.
3. Tony has wrote a scholarly ten-page essay.

> Look carefully at a few of the basic tense forms below:

Present	Past	Past Participle
go	went	gone
know	knew	known
write	wrote	written
deal	dealt	dealt

All the verbs in English in the past participle section of any grammar text must always be used with a helper—one of the verbs to be. The sentences above should read as follows:

* The children are/were/have/had gone to the store.
* Sandy is/was/had been known for her creativity in decorating sculptures.
* Tony has/had written a scholarly ten-page research paper (see any scholarly handbook or grammar book for more details and concrete examples).

Direction: In Exercises 26 to 30, noun-pronoun or verb errors may occur in some of the sentences. Follow the prompts in each section.

Exercise 26 Edit the sentences to create parallel antecedents. If no error occurs, write C beside the number

1. A conscientious student must be prepared to accept constructive criticism when his or her essays are reviewed by peers or professors.

2. During peer editing, a writer will get a number of suggestions that they may not appreciate but should always examine the relevance of the commentary to improve writing skills.

3. Some students are offended by professors' grades because they are unaware of the fundamental rules of English thus often write the way he or she speaks on a day-to-day basis.

4. A good writer must acknowledge that all writers make mistakes and that intellectual writing comes from extensive reading and constant writing, thus he or she should not be frustrated in the learning process.

5. Students seldom see the errors in their essays, as he or she might not spend enough time editing or they might not know what is wrong, or they might not know how to correct repetitive mistakes.

Exercise 27 Two of these sentences need noun-pronoun cohesion. Put an X beside the number, then rewrite it correctly. Now, put a check beside the correct sentences.

1. If one wants to achieve success, he or she must start making sensible decisions at an early age.

2. None of the players on the basketball team expected a new coach in the middle of the season.

3. Every one of the group members knows that he or she must be over twenty to be eligible to participate in the initiation ceremony.

4. Every child has a right to college education, though many parents cannot afford the cost of high tuition.

5. If global warming continues at its present rate, they will cause drastic changes in the ozone layers which climatologists contend will eventually create more severe temperature variation on earth, causing landforms to develop fault lines.

Exercise 28 Noun, pronouns, and verbs may not correspond. Rewrite correctly the sentences in which these errors occur. Do nothing where there is no error.

1. It is important for a parent to intervene before or when their children—young or old—become addicted to any drug, especially cocaine, heroin and marijuana.

2. Neither James nor his friends is prepared for the rigors of army training.

3. In America, everyone who is arrested should be read their Miranda Rights.

4. To survive in a changing economy and in the age of technological advancement, one must be flexible in accepting changes if they do not want to be stagnant in personal growth.

5. In court, everybody does not know that "Ignorance of the law is no excuse."

Exercise 29 Make all the nouns and pronoun antecedents plural. Write "no change" if there is no mistake. Be sure to check corresponding verbs.

1. Constitutionally, everybody is entitled to free speech, "life, liberty, and the pursuit of happiness," but they must be aware that with every privilege comes limitations.

2. A patriotic citizen often supports any movement or change that uplifts their country or community.

3. Peer critique enables students to get positive and negative feedback about their writing.

4. In Florida, as in most states, a seventeen year-old minor who commits a crime can and may be treated as an adult in the courts, depending on the crime he or she commits.

5. Not all adults are good role models, as some are thieves, pedophiles, murderers, and liars who are often a liability to society, with their bad influence.

Exercise 30 Most of the verbs in this set of sentences reflect tense shifting. Rewrite them correctly. Put "Correct" at the end of the sentences that need no change.

1. The surgeon elaborates, "Everyone of us are watching the chin protrude with the injected serum, and noticed how easy the process is."

2. When Jill began to look through the table of contents, she realizes the book have no information for her research paper.

3. The home owner's association charged the new residents an exorbitant fee of $550 per month for maintenance fee and justifies the cost to recent upgrades in particular residences.

4. The athletes display an excellent spirit of sportsmanship by congratulating their opponents, by agreeing to a luncheon, and invite them to their hometown.

5. Martin Luther King, Jr. and Mahatma Gandhi were committed to achieving peace, to demonstrating biblical principle of "turning the other cheek," and to inspiring goodness in humanity.

NOTES

Over-abused YOU, I, and WE

THE OVER-ABUSED "YOU"

Natalie Goldberg discusses clarity in writing and encourages students to be very clear to prevent the audience—reader—from being confused. In "Be Specific," she didactically tells practicing writers to "learn the names of everything" to provide leverage in using specific terms for objects, people, "plants, trees, flowers," and clear details such as the names of "birds, cheese, tractors, cars, building." This advice applies to overusing "you" in writing. More advanced writers only use the term when **it is absolutely necessary**. Remember that, in many cases, the issue, object, scenario that is being written about may not be applicable to all members of the audience. For example, if a speech is written to golf fans, the language may not be of interest to non-golf fans or to those who hate golf, but they must feel inclusive in the discussion (note my use of **discussion**, not tell, tell, tell, unless you are writing a process analysis essay or a report), so they too can be persuaded by the details. Furthermore, in formal writing, it is often inappropriate not to give "you" specificity. In fact, sometimes in identifying the audience as "you," the writer or speaker totally excludes himself or herself from the experience, so much so, that some readers may take offence—depending on what is being written. For example, imagine preachers who never admit that they sin yet frequently tell the congregation each Sunday or Saturday that they are "wretched sinners who need repentance." Would you not ask yourself if these preachers are exempt from repentance, if you believe in the Omnipotent Deity—God?

This rule also applies to non-clarity in using "<u>**it**</u>," "<u>**they**</u>," and "<u>**we**</u>." These words should only be used sparingly as antecedents—noun replacements, to avoid over-repeating subjects unnecessarily. Most importantly, essays are usually more interesting when specific names of objects, people, ideas are used (not vague terms like "it"; "they"; "we"; "the situation"; "whatever"; even "et cetera"). Overuse of these terms often leave readers frustrated, as they are indirectly asked to put in too many "fillers," which may or may not be what the writer intends to convey. Using specificity is like an eloquent and talented comedian entertaining an appreciative, cheering audience. Your essay should be no different. BE SPECIFIC! Paint an interesting mural with explicit words.

> Look carefully at this sentence:

  * You may not want to take a course in physics if you do not aspire to be a chemist.
    Note that the writer is excluded from this experience by the subject "you"
Here are two better ways to be inclusive of all readers
  * Those who aspire to become chemists need to take physics.
  * Prospective chemists must or should take physics.

> Now examine sentence 2.

  * Since you are parents, you must discipline your children.
The assumption here is that all the audience are parents, which may be false. A better way to target a general audience is to reconstruct the sentence to make it applicable to the parents, while making non-parents and the writer feel inclusive as well, as shown in the revised sentence below. Note also that in both examples, plural nouns and pronoun antecedents work better for conciseness and specificity.
  * Parents should discipline their children.

Exercise 31 (whole class exercise) Edit the sentences below either by restructuring or by substituting "you" and or "your" to let the writing be more audience-friendly with specificity of subject.

  1. If you wish to get an A in writing, you must be competent in the overall mechanics.

  2. You may become the target of your own gang, if you go against the group's ideologies or break the code of conduct.

  3. When you do not read instructions before carrying out a proven process, you tend to make mistakes by using "trial and error."

  4. When you do not work hard, you limit your capabilities.

  5. If you are given a task, do it to the best of your ability or you do not have to do it.

Exercise 32 **(warm-up exercises)** Replace "you" with a specific noun. Sentences may be reconstructed (optional).

1. You can avoid many mistakes, if you follow the wisdom of the elders.

2. More often than not, especially among educated peers, if you believe in necrophilia, necromancy, and voodoo, you will be ridiculed.

3. Most psychologists suggest that you should find your own path to happiness.

4. Should you have a heart attack, one suggestion is that you should take deep breaths in intervals.

5. Parents do not know if you will succeed or not, as the choices you make as young adults will often determine that.

Exercise 33 **(warm-up exercise)** In the sentences below, make the subjects clearer.

1. They are unsure whether it is the tomato or other vegetables that is causing the widespread salmonella poisoning in a number of states.

2. It is not the committee's priority.

3. If they want to win the competition, they will have to put in one hundred hours of practice.

4. You may be unaware that scientists usually test theories by conducting the same experiments repeatedly.

5. That is a very bad idea.

Exercise 34 Reconstruct each sentence eliminating any pronoun that is used as a subject, but do not change the original ideas. Phrases may be used as replacements, too.

1. We have to work hard to achieve success.

2. You can give back to the community by volunteering at the homeless shelter.

3. They often observe the behavior of animals in their natural habitat then write books to share their findings.

4. Doctors concur that it endangers the health of patients with diabetics 2.

5. Socrates, Buddha, and other renowned philosophers of all centuries encourage you to analyze all ideologies passed down as traditions as well as new notions.

Exercise 35 Write a descriptive essay (about 500 words) to intrigue to an audience. As you do so, try to avoid the words "you" and "your," if possible.

NOTES

Transitions

TROUBLESOME TRANSITIONS

N O GOOD WRITER CAN ever work without this list of tools—(words called transitions). As engineers, scientists, oceanographers, builders, other skilled-trades, and professionals need certain instruments or equipment to work well in their areas of expertise, so does everyone who wants to write well. Since transitions glue ideas and details together, they are absolutely necessary in any collegiate-level writing not only for cohesion but also to magnetize the readers. Without them, essays will be quite choppy and will jolt the readers like a driver being caught in a line of traffic—a traffic jam—(where each driver has to be constantly braking to avoid hitting the vehicle in front. Note that there are different transitions, outlined in the many handbooks. If the one your English professor recommends only focuses on documentation, buy a grammar book to study punctuation rules (governing transitions). A collegiate dictionary, with exemplary sentences, is a great help, too.

COORDINATING CONJUNCTIONS

> The coordination conjunction, the FANBOYS—(for, and, nor, but, or, yet, so), as a rule, are used as coordinators, though in informal or semi-formal writing they can be used to begin sentences. In formal writing, they link ideas, details, words, phrases, and sentences together. If **two independent clauses** are joined with any of the words in parenthesis), use a comma after the first sentence, as in the examples below:

* Civilization is reflective of a people's political, scientific, cultural, religious advancements within social institutions, **<u>yet</u>** in many third-world countries, growth of the people is minimal in the twenty-first century.

* In any setting, psychological studies point to the fact that people are intrinsically drawn together because of ethnocentricity, **<u>but</u>** some may view such groupings as overt prejudice against other races, which is not necessarily true.

> Note carefully the comma after sentence 1 in each example—followed by the coordinating conjunction. Note that **another independent sentence (clause)** follows the coordinator. This is when a comma is appropriately used with the FANBOYS.

> Now look at the same words—**yet** and **but**—without the comma in the sentences below. They join a (one) complete sentence—(an independent clause) to a fragment; therefore, no comma is needed. Apply the same rules when using any of the FANBOYS.

* Animal activists protest against mistreatment of animals **yet** to no avail.
    Independent Clause   **Fragment**
* America ensures individual freedom **but** not without limitations.
    Independent Clause   **Fragment**

Exercise 36 Make sentences using each of the coordinating conjunctions twice, with and without the comma. That means each word must be used to show that you understand both rules. If your professor does not assign this exercise, complete the assignment, then take it to the Writing Center on your campus to have it graded. You could also ask your English professor to check the punctuation for you, or ask a peer who is better at English to help compare your constructions with the examples above.

> Conjunctive adverbs and transitional phrases are excellent transitions to use in collegiate discussions, argumentative, and research essays, as they help to strengthen your viewpoints in conjunction with that of scholarly sources, but take caution in following the rules that govern.

Conjunctive Adverbs
    * also; anyhow; anyway; besides; consequently; finally; furthermore; hence; however; incidentally; indeed; instead; likewise; meanwhile; moreover; nevertheless; next; otherwise; similarly; still; then; therefore; thus

Commonly Used Transitional Phrases
    * after all; as a result; at any rate; at the same time; by the way; even so; for example in addition; in fact; in other words; in the first place; on the contrary; on the other hand

* Depending on sentence structures, as **a rule**, if they begin sentences, put a comma after them; if they are used to combine two independent sentences, put a semicolon after the first sentence and a comma after the conjunctive adverb; if they connect an independent clause and a fragment, put comma before and after the adverb.

> Look carefully at the examples, especially where the punctuations are underlined.

* **Consequently,** the large increase in the python population in the Everglades forces their extinction, as they endanger the lives of certain animals and humans.

* Drunk drivers have caused a number of accidents causing many deaths yearly; **therefore,** a law has been passed to curb the problem.

* Some plaintiffs think the justice system is unfair to certain ethnic groups, **hence** their disbelief in the courts.

Exercise 37 (**whole class warm-up exercise**) Put the correct punctuation at the appropriate places to prove that you understand the general rules when using the conjunctive adverbs and introductory phrases.

1. Environmentalists recommend taking care of the coral reefs to protect sea life however many polluters still dump garbage and poisonous pollutants into the sea and in landfills.
2. Despite the expense the committee wants to adopt ten more orphans.
3. Notwithstanding despite George's opposition to abortion, he supported his fiancée who had a brain tumor.
4. Many nature lovers, like Henry David Thoreau for example gravitate towards "the woods" to rejuvenate and de-stress the mind.
5. Success usually comes with perseverance nonetheless quite challenging

Exercise 38 Read the passage below, then, put in the appropriate punctuation used with the particular transition.

Pedophilia is a growing concern for most parents and concerned citizens. In fact studies show that since the 1980s, sexual abuse in children—both boys and girls, has been growing world-wide. In the local media for example almost daily, one child is abducted, raped, and sometimes forced to participate in pornographic filming. For instance on one of the American local talk shows, a victim's parent in disguise explains how the culprits force the child to have oral sex with a dog. Furthermore some parents sexually abuse their young children, too, and a number of studies prove that oftentimes relatives are the main perpetrators. As a result Congress passed Megan's Law to protect the innocent—children.

What does this law ensure? It relegates where sex offenders should live after they have served their prison sentences and sets limit to the proximity from any institutions where children are. Other stipulations include signing a registry in the town or city in which they reside. Studies show that pedophiles also have to give detailed personal information such as date of birth, crimes they commit, previous addresses and more when they register. Many nonetheless believe that the punishment is too stringent because most communities and employers treat them with disdain that some either become nomadic or live under bridges (if allowed by the state), like the homeless. On the other hand others agree that the extra punishment is necessary not only to protect children but also the community at large.

Exercise 39 Use as many of the following transitional phrases and words in a Comparison and Contrast essay. Try to finish in forty minutes or the time stipulated by the professor. As you write, focus on the standard punctuations reviewed (see pages 67–69). Edit carefully for misspellings, subject-verb disagreement, and write to appease your peers who may be critiquing your first draft.

1. anyhow
2. notwithstanding
3. on the other hand
4. similarly
5. hence
6. otherwise
7. consequently
8. incidentally
9. in addition
10. on the contrary

NOTES

Trite Expressions

TRITE VERBIAGE IS a mix of clichéd words, slang and regional phrases, idioms that serve no purpose in an essay but to add "padding," from a formal standpoint. The many students (whose first language is English) who use them explained that they were unaware that words we speak in non-academic settings are inappropriate in college writing. For example, if I say, "The cops busted the deceitful entrepreneur," I expect readers to visualize the police arresting a dishonest, corrupt person like Bernard Madoff. The word "busted" sounds interesting, but it is informal when used to mean "arrested." Terms such as "in my opinion; I am writing to tell you; I would like to say that; the truth of the matter; I can honestly say; I guess you can say; the next thing you know" borrowed from students writings are just a few of the myriad of informal expressions that are written as formal English in approximately ninety-five percent of college essays (i.e. in my composition classes). To those who want to write flowery terminologies, I suggest making up some new and unique ones that are unfamiliar to avid readers, but as a rule, most scholarly writers avoid them. Writing intellectually means expressing ideas as clearly as possible without dependence on these age-old adages. Remember, vocabulary is evolving as generations come and go, but what is in the dictionary defines the acceptable usages.

Directions: A number of the sentences in Exercises 40 to 43 may have expressions that are too flowery and are not needed to express the intended ideas. Follow the guidelines in the prompts.

Exercise 40 Reconstruct each sentence, eliminating all unnecessary verbiage. Do not change the concept expressed. First, identify the trite usages that should be deleted.

1. Let me tell you something: No child should ever be sexually abused.

2. I can write just fine.

3. Though the witnesses swore on the Bible that they saw the heist, it was not the truth from the get go.

4. I could not believe my eyes when I saw an alligator of that enormity basking in sun near the lake in front of my apartment.

5. The next thing you know, the driver swerves then hits the guard wall.

6. So you see, health insurance should be one of every tax payer's constitutional rights.

7. As a matter of fact, animals deserve proper treatment as humans.

8. To relieve stress on mother earth, cutting down forests must be curtailed.

9. Years down the road, climatologists predict that global warming will cause glaciers to melt causing Florida and New York City to be flooded like New Orleans.

10. As I was saying, sales of houses have declined in many states since 2007.

Exercise 41 Delete the words that are unnecessary to improve sentences more formally. Words may be added as long as the concepts expressed are not changed. Do nothing to sentences that have no informal verbiage.

1. I am writing to tell you about the new findings about Bracanalysis.

2. The money for the office party was spent way out of proportion

3. In my opinion, the legal system seems to be biased against certain ethnic groups.

4. Since that is my personal opinion, and we live in a Democracy, I should not be penalized.

5. I guess you can say that there is some goodness in human beings.

6. Believe it or not, many prescribed medicines affect the proper functioning of the central nervous system and other organs.

7. Back in the day, young people had more respect for the elderly and themselves.

8. If you "walk the walk and talk the talk" you are cool, if not, you are lame.

9. The nurse sat Jean down and explained the implications and procedures of having an abortion.

10. I would like to say, being young is no excuse for making so many foolish choices.

Exercise 42 Write the trite expressions and explain why each is unnecessary. Put "no change" at the end of those that are in standard form—collegiate writing.

1. For my conclusion, I want you to believe me, that the project took the life out of me, but it was worth it.

2. A positive attitude towards life affects our emotions and those around us.

3. What was killing me then, and is still killing me now, is their ingratitude.

4. To regain custody of her children, Brittany Spears went through hell and high water.

5. Marijuana is the name of the game

6. Right then and there, my brother and I knew that Dan was the murderer.

7. The little children were tumbling all over the place because their parents could not control them

8. Celebrities should be good role models, as young people emulate their behavior.

9. Before I knew it, the Girl Guides sold three hundred boxes of cookies.

10. As of now, there is no concrete evidence against the alleged arsonist.

Exercise 43 Which words are used informally in the sentences? Responses may be discussed in class.

1. The poodle is kind of cute and lovable.

2. We partied the night away.

3. Serena Williams overreacted and cursed expletives in the heat of the moment of impending loss of the US Open championship when the lines' person called "foot fault."

4. I had never seen anything like that in my life.

5. After losing the competition, Roger Federer refused to let it get the best of him.

6. Honestly speaking, I am telling the truth.

7. The party was sort of boring

8. The relationship amongst the siblings is starting to come around

9. You bet, the paparazzi took the picture despite the homosexual (gay) group's protest.

10. Lo and behold, Peter's mother gave him the surprise of his life, when she visited without notice.

Exercise 44 Rewrite these sentences replacing all trite expressions with standard phrasings. Circle all numbers where sentences need no revision.

1. The direction to Niagara Falls is right in front of you.

2. She walked in the job with her eyes wide open to the danger of espionage.

3. Traveling and internships allow one to learn what is out there.

4. Ida explains that she does not want to come off mean and insensitive.

5. When Jane learns of her backstabbing friends, she disassociates herself from the group.

6. When the burglars broke into our house, my heart almost jumped out of my chest.

7. Guys from around my way always call me snooty because I am ambitious.

8. Young people in lower-class neighborhoods seldom have good role models.

9. After the shots were fired, Paul exclaimed, "I am done in!"

10. The bullies' arrests were overdue, as they were asking for it.

NOTES

Word Bank:
Say Words

SAY VERBS

"The difference between the right word and the almost right word is the difference between the lightning and the lightning bug."

—Mark Twain

SINCE VERBS IGNITE life and meaning into essays, I have included this formal verb bank of "say" synonyms to help you transition into using more collegiate-level words to discuss ideas and issues throughout your studies. Twain alludes to the fact that the wrong word choices (not only verbs) can rob any piece of writing of its essence, especially when the views are wrapped in unnecessary phrasings or jargon, or the wrong words are used to express specific ideas; for example, I am board. Is this word used correctly? Does the writer want to write bored? What is distracting about this other sentence ideas? I am late because I was perambulating in the park and circumnavigating the area? Does the writer have to write in this circumlocutory (round-about) fashion? Would the sentence grab the audience better if "strolling" were used for perambulating? Is circumnavigating not related to the world instead of a park? This is exactly what I mean by using word choices that are unclear in order to sound intelligent. Euphemistic writing is antiquated (out-dated), especially in America, as even an educated audience expects a more realistic approach to writing. The general expectation is to let word usages be as close to standard speech in academia.

I reiterate; there is nothing wrong with using more collegiate-level words, but it is vital to get to the main points as concisely and as clearly as possible, with focus on appropriateness of verbs as well as other words. Most importantly, it is better to use a correct word that conveys a direct thought—that creates a specific imagery—than a long-winded phrase or sentence that means the same thing or one that is confusing. I recommend the use of a dictionary to ensure proper usage of unfamiliar "say" synonyms, especially in class, when the computer is not available to help with writing errors, though no one should depend solely on it, because whoever sets up the in-built programs does not know exactly what writers want to express. Be reminded that one of America's greatest orators, Malcolm X, taught himself word proficiency by using the dictionary on a daily basis, while being incarcerated. His rebirth of knowledge with the power of words increased so much that he shares this experience in "Coming to an Awareness of Language":

> I suppose it was inevitable that as my word base broadened, I could for the first time pick up a book and read and now begin to understand what the [writer] was saying. Anyone who has read a great deal can imagine the new world that opened. Let me tell you something: from then on until I left the prison, in every free moment I had, if I was not reading in the library, I was reading on my bunk. You couldn't have gotten me out of books with a wedge. Between Mr. Mohammed's teachings, my correspondence, my visitors ... and my reading of books, months passed without my even thinking about being imprisoned. In fact, up to then, I never had been so truly free in my life.
>
> —qtd. in Paul Eschholz and Alfred Rosa, "Coming to an Awareness of
> Language"

In discussion, to keep ideas current and fresh, the present tense and active voice are often more effective, though this depends on what is being written about. For example, when discussing literature, Modern Language Association (MLA) and other writing disciplines encourage the use of present tense. In research and argumentative essays, the present tense also gives more realism—more relevance—to the writing, to interpretation, and to discussion per se. For these reasons, I have intentionally put the verbs in the present, because too often, too many students write all their essays in the past. This can create disinterest or boredom, if the assignment is not a narrative. Remember to choose wisely from the six forms: present; past; future; present perfect; past perfect; future perfect (which also have variations). Study the recommended handbook to avoid switching from tense to tense (see page 45). Focus also on subject-verb agreement, as in the examples below whenever you write and speak formally.

Example 1:
　The **principal acclaims** the graduates for their high scholastic achievements.
　singular subject + singular verb

Example 2:
　The **principals acclaim** ...
　plural subject + plural verb

Expand Your Repertoire of Synonyms for "Say"					
acclaims	advocates	announces	articulates	avers	
accounts	affirms	answers	ascertains	avows	
accuses	agrees	apologizes	ascribes	----------	
addresses	airs	opposes	asks	----------	
adds	alleges	approves	asserts	----------	As
admits	alludes	arbitrates	assures	----------	
admonishes	amplifies	argues	attests	----------	
advises	analyzes	arouses	authorizes	----------	
backbites	belittles	blames	blurts	broadcasts	
babbles	bellows	blares	boasts	browbeats	
banters	berates	blasphemes	brags	----------	Bs
begs	beseeches	blasts	briefs	----------	
belabors	bewails	bleats	broaches	----------	
calls	cites	compels	confides	converses	
canonizes	claims	complains	confides	conveys	
cautions	clarifies	compliments	confirms	convinces	
challenges	classifies	concludes	congratulates	corresponds	
chants	coerces	concurs	connotes	corroborates	Cs
charges	commands	concedes	consents	counsels	
cheers	comments	confers	consults	criticizes	
chimes	communicates	confesses	contends	critiques	
cross-examines	curses	----------	----------	----------	
debates	decries	delivers	diagnoses	----------	
debriefs	decrees	demands	digresses	----------	
declaims	defends	denies	disagrees	----------	
declares	defies	denotes	disclaims	----------	Ds
declassifies	delegates	denounces	discusses	----------	
declines	deliberates	describes	disputes	----------	
decrees	delineates	designates	drawls	----------	

educates	encourages	establishes	explicates	----------	
elaborates	endorses	evaluates	exposes	----------	
elucidates	enlightens	exaggerates	expostulates	----------	Es
embellishes	enquires	exalts	expounds	----------	
emphasizes	enunciates	exonerates	expresses	----------	
familiarizes	forbids	foretells	forewarns	formulates	Fs
----------	----------	----------	----------	frames	
generalizes	guesses	guides	----------	----------	Gs
hypothesizes	----------	----------	----------	----------	Hs
illuminates	implicates	infuses	interjects	interviews	
illustrates	imposes	insists	interprets	intimates	Is
implants	indicates	instructs	interrogates	introduces	
implies	informs	intercedes	interrupts	invokes	
judges	justifies	----------	----------	----------	Js
labels	laments	lectures	lists	litigates	Ls
maintains	mediates	misguides	misinforms	misquotes	Ms
----------	----------	----------	----------	misreports	
notes	notifies	----------	----------	----------	Ns
objects	opposes	orders	outlines	overstates	Os
paraphrases	pledges	posits	presents	proposes	
persuades	points out	postulates	professes	purports	Ps
pinpoints	poses	predicts	pronounces	----------	
queries	questions	quotes	----------	----------	Qs
rationalizes	recites	rejects	replies	retells	
reasons	recounts	remarks	reports	retracts	
reasserts	refers	remonstrates	reproaches	reveals	
reassures	refutes	renders	reproves	reverberates	Rs
rebuts	reinforces	renounces	responds	reviews	
recaps	reiterates	repeats	restates	----------	
says	sermonizes	solicits	states	stresses	
sensationalizes	showcases	speaks	stipulates	suggests	Ss
talks	tells	teaches	testifies	translates	Ts
verbalizes	verifies	vilifies	voices	vouches	Vs
whines	----------	----------	----------	----------	Ws

NOTES

Writing Errors (commonly made)

WRITING ERRORS TO AVOID

I T WOULD BE A Herculean task to cover all the errors students make in college writing, and I am sure I have missed quite a number of dictionary inclusions, but the focus here is to help inexperienced writers avoid these actual words and phrases that are written in essays too often, as standard or formal English, even by students who have already passed Composition 101. In this section, most of the words are colloquialisms (informal usages—acceptable in normal day-to-day speech, but unacceptable in writing—unless in dialog or placed in quotation marks for emphasis), while some are slang usages (used only by particular in-groups but are inappropriate in writing, and in polite company). Others are standard English which are often misused. All professors expect formality in essays (except in creative writing), and the audience will appreciate clarity rather than having to guess the writer's (your) intended meanings.

Not all readers are familiar with certain regional expressions. For example, those whose first language is British English might think of small goats or young children under five years old, if they read the word "kids." Others might think of those under fifteen. In America, however, the age may vary from babies to older adults—(depending on the age of the parent or person who is speaking). Others might not know what "cops" mean, as some are accustomed to calling all police—(male and female) "policeman" or police; some might not know that the term "you guys" is referring both males and females. Again, to many influenced by European English, "guy" might only be the informal synonym for man, while for others, depending on the culture, the word represents "a man in old clothes" being burned on a fire during Guy Fawkes Night or Bonfire Night's celebration, (historically shown to be upheld in England, New Zealand, South Africa, and a few areas in the Caribbean) on November 5, yearly, as a reminder of the thwarting of the Catholic terrorists' plan to bomb the House of Parliament in London in 1605). Do some research on Guy Fawkes, if this is of interest.

These are a few reasons universal usages are necessary; moreover, regional language must be avoided in standard writing, at all times, in order to relate to a global audience. Apart from these expectations, it is important to write as reader-friendly as possible, as all good writers write to impress the audience, not so much themselves. Remember never to write for the professor alone. Imagine that your essay will be read world-wide—to that larger audience.

Taking a dictionary to class is to your advantage to familiarize yourself, if unsure about terminologies that may be non-standard, especially during in-class writing. Surprisingly, from semester to semester, some students are shocked to realize that what they thought was standard is not. Throughout, I have asked a number of questions to encourage active participation to persuade you to think about the impact of every word, phrase, or sentence whenever you write and read, as I have done in this workbook. Let your voice be heard as you focus on clear explanations in the exercises and in discussion in the essays to capture the audience. The suggested explanations in keys are only suggestions. Remember, you are the only one who know the ideas circling within your subconscious, and I implore you to write the truth from that place in any essay while abiding by the generic rules of the discipline that the professor wants (e.g. Modern Language Association—MLA; American Psychological Association—APA or other).

--ace: (informal when used to mean successful or do well): e.g. ace a test. It is better to explain that you passed the test with a high score or that you got an A or B+.

--acronyms: Write out full meaning when first used, and abbreviate in subsequent use, even if abbreviated letters do not form words like AIDS (acquired immune deficiency syndrome); Palm Beach Community College (PBCC); United States of America (U.S.A. or USA—now acceptable without the periods or full stops).

--ain't: (very informal) Use "am not/ is not/are not" in standard writing and speech.

--alright: (informal)—never written together—all right (correct usage).

--a lot of: (informal when used to refer to countable or non-countable nouns: Use specific terms such as many, a number of, several, much, a large quantity, etc.).

--amount versus number: Use amount with non-countable things (e.g. money, water, sugar, meat, etc.) and number with countable objects (e.g. people, trees, animals, etc).

--antsy: (informal when used for cannot be still or restless, restive, agitated, etc.)

--arm candy: definitely informal for a beautiful woman/wife used mostly as an object to augment a man's status, usually males/husbands in prestigious positions

--artsy: Find another way to describe those who love the arts or who are artistically talented.

--auntie or aunty: These terms are endearing to use in person but informal to write for aunt, unless used **as a name**. In that case, capitalize beginning—Auntie Carol.

--back in the day: What time is this? Be specific. Give a time period—prehistoric times; ancient times; fourth century BC; 1800s; 1950s? State an exact period or era.

--bad-mouth: Use criticize, or talk about, or similar synonym.

--bamboozle: Use trick, deceive, swindle, or other formal synonyms

--barf: Why not use vomit—a standard usage.

--basket case: Crazy, irrational, insane, psychopath, illogical, foolish are a few standard, synonyms—depending on the level of the behavior.

--behind: colloquial when used for buttocks

--bellyache: unacceptable for stomach ache

--belly button: navel (standard usage)

--bellyful: full stomach

--between versus among: Use the former to compare two, the latter to compare more than two.

--Big Apple: New York City is better. If "Big Apple" is used, it must be placed in quotation marks and the proper term must be explained in the context of the sentence or paragraph, too.

--big bucks: large sums of money

--binge: informal as a noun—"to go on a binge": to eat or drink sporadically when not hungry is one way to explain the meaning

--bitch about something/somebody; labeling a person bitch; calling life a bitch: All are colloquialisms. The first cannot be used for fussing/quarrelling/gossiping, or for being upset; the second is an inappropriate label for a female no matter how low her morals or how degrading her behavior; the third implies that there are challenges, struggles, trials, tribulations that are inevitable as one matures. Notice the clarity of thought in the explanations given that makes the reader understand clearly.

--blinders—Putting on blinders: biased views—refusing to think objectively; pretending not to understand; failing to understand—more collegiate phrasings

--breather—take a breather: rest or relax; take some deep breaths

--brown-nose: This is a slang for trying to be extremely polite and attentive to the "powers that be," for example, your professor to get a good grade, or your employer in order not to be fired when you are habitually late or to cover your inefficiency on the job.

--brushing off someone: Do you mean ignore, rebuff, disregard or similar synonym? A phrase can also be as effective as one word, too.

--buddy or bud: How easy it is to write or say friend!

--busted: No such word! Burst (present), burst (past), burst (past participle) are basic tense forms. "Busted" cannot be used for being arrested, or for an open wound gained by falling, or for being hit.

--bust-up: Why not use disagreement for a broken friendship or marriage? Why not say the police dispersed the crowd by using tear gas?

--busty: Do you mean large breast? Write just that.

--butter up: This term is to feign affection for selfish gain. Is this a common human tendency to give false compliment or praise to others? I often wonder. Do you think this is done for survival, or is this behavior conscious hypocrisy?

--contractions: Avoid them in formal writing. Write the words out. In that way, you will not make the mistake of writing "it's" (it is) for " its" (replacement for the noun), or "they're" (they are) for "there are" and other commonly misused contractions, especially the homonyms.

--conversate: There is no such word; the proper verb is converse.

--cool: non-standard when used to mean accepting bad behavior or fashion as the norm--e.g. 1. Covering the body with tattoos is pretty cool, so my friends and I plan to do so. 2. My parents are very cool; they never discipline me when I do something wrong.

--co-op: This term is inappropriate for any cooperative group. It is better to specify the place in question, for example, Beach Front Enterprises.

--cop: Please say police or police officer in a class setting.

--could of: Never write "of," but <u>have</u> (same as would <u>have</u>; should <u>have</u>).

--couple of: Couple means <u>two</u> in formal English. Avoid couple of days, weeks, months, years ago. If you mean two, six, fifty, say so. Be specific.

--crap—talking crap: Do you mean talking nonsensically, talking foolishly, using ludicrous or absurd argument?

--cuff: Never use cuff for arrest in formal writing or speaking.

--cut to the chase: Do you mean get to the point, as you should do to avoid wordiness?

--cute: Maybe the individual is quite handsome (male) or beautiful (female), or maybe it is your favorite pet, but cute is always informal to describe the individual or the object.

--dead wrong: Avoid this trite verbiage. Find a standard word for a lapse in judgment or a lack of insight. These two phrases are better for any academic writing.

--due to. Do not use "Due to" to begin a sentence. Owing to is a better option, or restructure the sentence, putting one of the **verbs to be** before the phrase (e.g. has been due to; was due to; have been due to; were due to, etc) Study correct usage in this sentence: The growing unemployment rate **is due** to the dire economic recession that causes employers to lose clientele (see recommended handbook or a dictionary for additional examples).

--etc.: (et cetera): Note how often I spell the formal usage (et cetera) throughout the workbook to get it correctly into your subconscious. In fact, it is always better to give a clear list.

--English: English is always written with a capital E.

--Every day versus everyday: Learn when to use the compound form (see examples): a. Every day Joe goes to work. b. Going to work is an everyday fulfillment for Joe.

--exam: acceptable, but examination is more formal

--face-off: Do not be impressed by the sound. Be specific. Do you mean people competing for a prize, or are they arguing, or is there a fight, or is it a confrontation among or between factions? Note how the reader could misinterpret the writer's intended meaning, especially if the context is not clearly detailed.

--finally and lastly: As a rule, leave these words for the concluding paragraph. You should not tell your audience "finally/lastly," then write two or more paragraphs before the concluding one in your essays. Once those words are read, the reader is ready for the closing, just like the prosecution in a courtroom giving the closing remarks before the jury decides the verdict.

--fun time: to have <u>fun time</u>? Isn't this phrase more like a Grade 3 child's writing? Find a more collegiate term like pleasurable, enjoyable, or other.

--Generalizations: Generalized statements/facts that cannot be proven must be avoided or covered with some scholarly source or term. e.g. Sentence 1: <u>Doctors report</u> or <u>studies show</u> that sexually transmitted disease and Swine Flu are on the rise in the United States. Note how the facts are supported by scholarly coverage (underlined).

* Look at sentence 2: Americans are obese because they eat too much fast food. The last statement is certainly not true, as not all Americans eat fast food; neither are all Americans obese. This kind of writing lacks objectivity and must be avoided.

--gonna: This may sound exciting to fit in with peers but certainly not exciting where formality is expected

--goof around: What about wasting time, idling, not taking life seriously!

--guy: man, male, gentleman, boy—standard meanings

--gym: Go to the gym, but write gymnasium (formal) in essays, unless it is a dialog.

--graduate high school/college: No! No! graduate from! This phrase is so embedded in many students' sub-consciousness that writing "graduate **from** high school/college" (the correct usage) is often a problem.

--grouse: Are you constantly complaining about someone, about anything, everything, or over a particular matter of concern over and over because you are upset? Then, you do have a grouse, but in these cases the word is informal.

--hang out: socialize, spend time with

--hang about: to loiter where one should not be

--had went: (wrong) This phrase is a very popular faulty grammar. When **has**, or **have**, or **had** is used before the verb, use the past participle, not the past tense, unless the past tense is the same as the past participle in example 2: has/had/have gone (not went); has/had/have brought (not bring); e.g. 2. has/had/have run (not ran).

--high school: These two words are always separate, and the "h" and "s" should never be capitalized unless the name of the school is mentioned, for example, Boynton Beach High School.

--hisself: No such word! The correct word is himself.

--in today's society: This phrase is too "high school-like" for college writing. Moreover, it is too general to be inclusive of all societies, since the issue of discussion may not be relevant to all areas of the world. For example, is malaria or Down's syndrome on the rise in all societies? Do the same cultural rules govern all communities and countries? Maybe "today" alone could suffice to cover the fact being discussed, or it is better to be more specific: in twenty-first century America; modernized society; civilized societies; third-world countries, in the modern era, or similar coinage.

--just about: cannot be used for almost, nearly.

--kids: Avoid all regional language; they are unacceptable in formal writing, because all isoglosses have different ways/jargon of expressing the same idea, so everyone is never familiar with all the phrases and terminologies that people from different regions use. For example, in American contest, most parents call their children kids, no matter the age, but this is not universal.

--lab: The best place to go for help with writing weaknesses is the writing lab on the college campus, but do not be surprised if the tutors tell you to change lab to laboratory (more formal usage—depending on the kind of essay).

--laid and laid up: Do not use the former for having sex and the latter for getting pregnant or being sick in bed.

--mad at someone or at oneself: Mad means crazy in formal English, not angry or upset.

--me and my brother: Put self last in speaking and writing: My brother and I or my brother and me—**depending on the sentence** (test I and me with the verb to determine which to use).

--many: Use with countable nouns (e.g. objects that can be counted: stones, people, trees, cars, sandwiches, et cetera.).

--mind-boggling: Have you ever been guilty of using this word as formality? Explore the dictionary for yourself to become more familiar with standard and non-standard words. A few synonyms for mind-boggling are incredible, unbelievable, unimaginary.

--mines: Never say "it is mines." It is mine is correct. Mines is the plural of mine, the place where minerals are mined like coal, bauxite ore (see dictionary).

--much: Use with things that are inseparable—non-countable objects (e.g. water, dirt, milk, sugar).

--nice: Avoid using nice for something that cannot be tasted. What exactly is meant when we say a person is nice? Is the individual caring, generous, loving, considerate, pleasant, optimistic, et cetera? Describe the specific traits. Do not ask the audience to determine the meaning for you. When referring to food, explain with terms like delicious, palatable, appetizing, or other concrete synonyms. Nice is too abstract.

--off of: Look at these sentences: a. Take the dishes off of the table. b. James is coming off of two weeks vacation. Does the "of" serve any purpose in these sentences? Do the meanings change without the "of"? Is the "of" necessary?

--okay; O.K. (both informal) "All right" is a good replacement.

--out there: "Programs are out there; something is out there." Where is this place? You must give a more definitive explanation.

--party pooper: What exactly does this mean? Going to many parties, hosting parties, going to parties frequently? Say exactly which you mean in formal English.

--picky: Do you mean to be selective, hard to please, or to be overly fastidious?

--pretty much: What is "pretty" about "much"? Use a standard term similar to exactly, as is, to be certain, more than likely, absolutely, certainly, or other.

--prof. When setting up the heading of your papers, use the full term professor, and if you do not have a very close relationship with the professor, avoid the term, too, when addressing him or her.

--pros and cons: Advantages and disadvantages are formal replacements.

--the reason why or the reason is because: Never write **why** or **because** after "the reason is." Both are informal and redundant. Formal examples:—The reason many people are successful is **that** they work hard (get directly to the point), or use **that** after reason: Sentence 2: The reason **that** many people are successful is through hard work.

--return back: This is redundant. If someone returns, that person comes/goes back.

--reverses back: another redundancy—If someone reverses (more collegiate) or backs up a vehicle/a car, in which direction is the driver going?

--riled up: Use words that are synonymous to angry, irritated.

--scatter brain: Do you mean disorganized, foolish, forgetful? Since labels destroy people's self esteem, why not encourage positivism, anyway?

--sexist usage: Avoid using male coinages to relate to females, such as man, mankind. policeman, post or mailman, spokesman, and others. Your word choice must acknowledge both sexes, if that is your intended meaning. For example, add to old adages using square brackets: [Hu]man, or change word form: humanity; human beings; people when referring to both sexes.

--schmuck. Stupid and foolish are more scholarly. Moreover, it is more civil to avoid labels (formal or informal) that belittle others.

--scumbag: dirty; unclean; unkempt

--screw up: A simply replacement is "make a mistake."

--screwed up: made a mistake or abnormal behavior patterns

--scrounge off: Do you mean to depend on others for financial support, to take advantage of someone's kindness, to continuously beg or solicit help from the others?

--scrumptious: Do you mean tasty or delicious?

--slacker: Is this person lazy or a non-productive citizen in a community?

--sleazy: Would untrustworthy, unkempt, dishonest convey your intended meaning?

--standoffish: Boastful, arrogant, conceited are more formal.

--stats: Use statistics instead when writing formally.

--stick with somebody or something is non-standard. Words like support, work with, agree with or to, or your own phrasing are more appropriate.

--stuff: Stuff used to mean things or objects is unacceptable as standard. Are you talking about all the clothes, handbags, shoes, jewelry, and baseball hats that are left on the bed as you hasten to get to class and work on time? Are you referring to all the accouterments in the trunk of your vehicle or in the garage? Write the exact name for whatever is being written about or use a collective word like "accouterments" that covers the intended subject(s) because "stuff" is standard when used as a verb or adjective, as shown below in these two sentences:

    1. Stuff the seasoning inside of the turkey, so it can marinate overnight.

    2. The seasoning stuffed in the turkey gave the meat a delicious flavor.

--their: To use this word correctly, put a noun after it to show possession: their cars; their house; their children; their friends; their ancestors; their siblings.

--theirselves: No such word! Use themselves.

--thru: Do not worry about the sign at fast-food restaurants. "Thru" should not be used for "through."

--till: Are you talking tilling the soil, or did you intend to write until? Be reminded **not to** use till for until—standard usage.

--twenty-four seven: twenty-four hours per day; every day; often (few standard terms)

--Umpteen/umpteenth time: Cannot be used for many or a number of!

--Uncle Sam: United States of America, or The States, or U.S.A. (USA without the periods is also acceptable now).

--Uncle Tom: If used symbolically to indicate master-slave relationship—Blacks who display more allegiance to Caucasians than to their own race, put quotation marks around (" "), but it is better to explain intended meaning clearly to avoid offending the reader.

--uncool: Do you mean those who do not share a group's or individual's values and ideals: the misfits; the rebels; the dissidents; the nonconformists reflected in Emily Dickinson's "Much Madness is divinest Sense—"?

--Under-the-counter: illegal

--under-whelmed/underwhelming: unimpressed; disinterested; unconvinced; uninterested—a few standard replacements

--unfazed: When this word is used, does it show nonchalance —"I do not care" attitude or a lack of shock or surprise, being unimpressed by the action, event, or person, good or bad?

--upper crust: Formal synonyms—upper class; the bourgeoisie; bourgeois group; elites; capitalist; the ruling class

--uppity: Is the person displaying high self-esteem? Conceit? Arrogance? Pomposity? Define the term you wish to convey.

--uptight: easily annoyed; miserable; tense; anxious —what exactly do you want to say?

--pricey: very expensive

--veggie: better to write vegetables or list some—carrots, peas, lettuce, tomatoes, okra, cabbage, garlic, and others.

--very fun: In any college-level writing, no professor expects to read: "It was very fun." The writer most likely means that something is enjoyable, pleasurable, or exciting.

--vibes: can be formal but not when the emotion is not expressed, as someone giving off particular vibe! Explain what that mood is, for example: somber, jovial, positive; pessimistic, cordial, detached, unpleasant, happy, et cetera.

--wasted: Do not use for drunk.

--weirdo: (see whacky)

--what not or whatever: Mention all the examples possible, or use et cetera (not etc).

--wimp: Perhaps, we all are wimps in one way or the other. How many people have all these qualities: strength; bravery; confidence? Maybe, we should assess our weaknesses and strengths before labeling those we deem inferior in human traits. Do you agree or disagree?

--zap: Informal when used for slap or hit.

--zit: Do you mean pimple?

--whacky: Do you mean eccentric, crazy?

--wimp: one who shows cowardice all the time, lacks bravery

--wing it: Should a student "wing" a class presentation? No, a well-prepared presentation will make the speaker seem more intelligent, thus earn a better grade from peers and professors. Lack of preparation forces the presenter to ramble (called ad lib) with "aahm, aahm" or to fumble with the paper, thus distract the audience. It is better to prepare and to study the main points (if the paper is not going to be read) than to "wing it," especially if you are not yet as articulate as you would want to be.

--wuss: (slang) Not a good idea for a coward!

--yap: Extremely talkative individuals tend to be poor listeners. Do you agree?

--yep: How polite to answer, yes!

--yucky: Do you mean an eerie feeling, unpleasant, unpalatable?

--yummy: What a way to say delicious, luscious, delectable, and tasty! The word "yummy" makes readers want to taste that pie, eat that chicken leg, but it is informal.

NOTES

Other Errors to Avoid

OTHER TERMINOLOGIES TO AVOID

As the English language evolves with generational vocabulary changes and words either become obsolete or are adapted, confusion as to what is standard can result. For these reasons, this section covers additional (but not all) informal terminologies that are in the *Oxford Advanced Learner's Dictionary*, many that are often spoken during presentations and sometimes written. Unfortunately, academia does not recognize these usages in polite company, just as one's character is judged by the merits of one's behavior. If your purpose is to write and speak intelligently, then much is expected from the language that you use. For example, how would you view a professor who speaks dialect or slang at every session he or she meets the class? Would you lose respect for that individual? Would you expect our global leaders and ambassadors to talk with colloquialisms, clichés, and slang? How would they be viewed? The same expectations apply to all students who enter college. Most likely, professors will not judge you, but all expect each individual to grow academically by adapting to college-writing expectations and by showing understanding.

What is adapting to college expectations, and how is understanding shown? This means that regarding class assignments, academic language is expected, especially in writing. Here Charles Darwin's theory "Survival of the Fittest" becomes applicable, as your main focus is to prove competency in the expected language, which is American English in America and British English outside of the United States. Remember that while there are universal similarities, there are variations in both, especially in word choice—vocabulary. To ensure universality, the disciplines of Modern Language Association (MLA), American Psychological Association (APA), and Chicago style mandate certain guidelines, which are not optional. In all styles, conformity to English standards is expected. Though oral speech has its own phrasings and affords more laxity, it is never "kosher" to be too "cool," when speaking in an educated setting, because the art of speaking well is equally as important. Notice that I have placed the two words, used colloquially, in quotation marks to substantiate the point that informalities are used for emphasis. Seeing the symbols (" "), the audience automatically knows that the words are used consciously or intentionally, as in a "Roast" (a method of celebrating someone's achievements by using mostly negative humor to create laughter—to entertain that individual as well as the audience).

> Note: Your definitions do not have to be worded exactly as mine, and I recommend that you peruse the dictionary, like Malcolm X when he was incarcerated, to increase your knowledge of both formal and informal words. I, too, am on this same mission.

A creature of habit: suggestive of inability to change habits—usually bad ones

Addressing the issue head on: telling the truth though others may be offended

A different story: irrelevant to the issue being discussed

As good as gold: an antiquated simile that connotes that one is almost perfect

Ask someone to come around: when you give an open invitation to someone to visit your home any time

At the top of your game: doing something with excellence—to the best of one's ability

A touchy subject—controversial discussions that cause others to be upset, as religion

Bad blood in the family: to be in constant disagreement with relatives

Bad blood on your hands: to murder/kill someone

Bang your head against the wall: failing to get others to accept or acknowledge your views

Basket case: one who has lost the ability to think rationally

Bite your tongue: not commenting; giving no response

Bring home the bacon: the person who works to maintain the family

Beyond my wildest dreams: unexpected fortune, success, results

Blood, sweat and tears: to try very hard; to put much effort into what is being done to achieve goals

Boggles the mind: too much to comprehend, or to think about, or to decide what to do

Brush it off: pretending that something does not bother you by ignoring the issue; show no care; have no interest in something, disinterested

Cabbie: taxi driver

Call: informal when used to mean it is one's turn to give one's view, usually to decide on a matter when others are indecisive

Champ: champion

Champing at the bit: to be anxious to do something

Chances are that: it is more likely that, or it is likely to

Chancy: hazardous; dangerous to do

Chip shop: a place where fish and potato chips are served in England as a take-out meal similar to McDonald's value meal

Carry on: quarrelling continuously with a bad attitude

Case the joint: observe the layout of a place to go back to steal

Cat's whiskers or py'jamas (BrE); pajamas (US) to be overly pompous or conceited

Character—he/she is a character: should not used to label a person who has a trait or habit (not necessarily a bad one) that makes him or her unique

Chatty: extremely talkative, but friendly

Chimp: chimpanzee

Chink: a rude (slang) label to call one of Chinese origin

Christmassy: referring to the joy felt during the Christmas season itself, coupled with the beauty of the decorations along with the cheerful nature of many people

Chintzy: anything that looks very cheap

Chummy: pleasant to be around

Chump: stupid

Cinch: not difficult; an easy task; a behavior that is expected of someone e.g. Mohammed Ali when he was a prime boxer or Tiger Woods in golf competitions

City slicker: having certain stereotypical attitude of those who are raised in the city, as a "New Yorker" who wears certain Parisian fashion and speaks with a distinct accent

Civvies: (slang) apparel worn by military personnel when not on duty—civilian clothing

Clan: a family with many children; a group (e.g. Amish) linked together but not biologically

Clean bill of health: when the medical report shows that all the organs are working well

Clean up your act: changing one's behavior for the better

Clear out: similar to spring cleaning when people get rid of things that crowd the house, usually at a garage sale or via charity

Clincher: usually an idea given to bridge communication when no one wants to make the final decision, or finding a solution at the right time—to spark communication especially when there is an awkward silence in a group

Clip something off: shorten time allotted to complete a task, usually to have time for leisure

Clout: to slap someone or something very hard with the hand

Clue somebody in: to update the person about important information or the latest gossip

Clued up: being aware of certain information about something or someone

Cockamamie: incredible news or story

Cockeyed: could mean crooked—(like clothes on a hanger) but usually connotes a silly plan that is bound to fail

Coke: cocaine

Con: to deceive or swindle—usually out of money or to get some favor

Condo: condominium

Contacts: lenses worn directly over the pupils—contact lenses

Cook something up: make up false accusation or excuse

Cook the books: like an accountant/tax preparer/entrepreneur who changes the numbers to cheat for the client or for himself/herself

Cook somebody's goose: prevent that person from succeeding

Cotton on to something: to fully understand by one's intrinsic knowledge

Cotton up to someone: to try to be more sociable

Crabby: a horrible person, usually very miserable and annoying

Cracker: (informal when used as a racial stereotype to demean someone) usually refers to an uneducated, poor Caucasian

Crackerjack: a very good, jovial, considerate person; a good thing

Crack of dawn: close to daylight

Crashing the party: going when not invited

Crazy: not acting sensibly or rationally (always informal when used an adjective or noun especially in the US e.g. crazy schedule; making me go crazy; crazy as hell)

Creep: usually someone who irritates you by his or her presence

Creepy: to have an eerie feeling about a thing or person

Crowd-pleaser: an entertainer (e.g. Michael Jackson) who loves acknowledgement from the crowd on and off the stage

Crowd-puller: anyone or anything that attracts attention.

Crybaby: one who is extremely thin-skinned and does not take even constructive criticism well

Cuckoo: informal when used to mean not of sound mind or behavior may be abnormal

Cuddly: irresistible—like a little poodle or a newborn that you want to hold, love, and kiss

Cutting class: not attending intentionally

Cutesy: a person who is very focused on physical appearance and mode of dress that draw excessive attention

Dead give away: very obvious; something that is clearly seen or understood

Doggone: a show of frustration when something goes wrong

Dopey: foolish

Dressing down: to talk to someone in a condescending manner

Dressed to kill: overdressed for the occasion

Dressed to the nines: overly dressed in formal attire

Druggie: one who takes too much drugs—legally and illegally

Dump: where garbage is thrown

Dumping someone: to sever a relationship—intimate or platonic

Dumping your problems on others; constantly complaining

Eager beaver: a person who is always doing something

Egg-head: a very intelligent person who enjoys studying

Exec: means executive

Eye something up: to show interest in; to admire a person sexually

Fabulous: not formal when used to describe people or activity

Face the music: Prepare to take the consequences for your actions.

Fag: offensive to call a homosexual this, usually done by those who are homophobic

Failure to connect the dots: not recognizing the warning signs

Fall for something: to be gullible; believing without analyzing or examining the plan/concept/idea

Fanatic: one who has an extreme view and is seldom rational

Fanny: (slang) cannot be used for buttocks or vagina in formal writing

Fed: should not be used for Federal Bureau of Investigation (FBI)

Feeling funny: not well; sick

Fire away: start speaking; your time to talk

First base: failure to start a project; failing to initiate a closer sexual relationship

Flabby: unacceptable to describe one who has lost much weight thus has loose skin as the elderly who have lost firmness in the muscles

Flighty: is not conscientious, usually naïve; immature

Flip-flop: (not the slippers) indecisive; cannot make up your mind; easily changes opinion in minutes, especially when confronted
Fluke: successful unexpected happening like winning the lottery

Fishy: having a suspicion that something is not right

Frame-up: to tell untruths about a person to get that individual in trouble, especially with the police, or employer, or family

Folk(s): people

Footsie: playing with someone's feet under the table, usually to flirt

Forty winks: get a short nap

Freak: someone who has unusual fetishes

Freaky: abnormal behavior from the norm

Freebie: free handouts usually given by companies to promote their products and to boost sales

Freeze someone out: ignore the person

Fusspot: a fastidious individual

Gabfest: women friends gathering to share latest news—gossip

Game: informal when used as a trick to win one's opponent; a plan of action to ensure that you are the victor

Gang: when used as a group of bad people who terrorize others

Gang up on someone: joining with others to accost another person

Gang-bang: (slang) when the whole group or some of its members rape an individual

Gangbusters: energetic individual, usually young people or the young-at-heart

Gas-guzzler: a vehicle that uses the gas quickly

Gas man: a person who goes to other people's house to check the gas lines if there is a problem

Gawk: bad manners to stare at other people

Geriatric: offensive to the elderly or aged

Get-up: unusual, unorthodox mode of dressing—unlike the fashion trend of the era

Give away: things given away as charitable gifts

Ghastly person: unacceptable word for someone you do not like

Glob: like a drop of ink, water, paint on a canvas, a raindrop

Glop: "a thick red substance that looks, tastes, and feels unpleasant"

Gnarly: slang for "very good; excellent"

Go bonkers: to become crazy

Go with somebody: to have sex with someone who is not necessarily your legal spouse; to have an intimate relationship

Gob: mouth; "shut your gob"—an informal way to tell someone that he or she talks too much

Gobs: lots of something—money, froth in the mouth, bubbles

God-awful: a terrible mistake

Gofer: an employee who does the odd jobs for people in his or employ

Goggle: to look wide-eyed at someone—to stare at the individual with a sense of surprise

Go-getter: one who will surmount any obstacle to achieve his or her goals and aspirations

Go-go: a period of time when businesses thrive

Goings-on: illegal or suspicious activities

Going-over something: scrutinizing with intensity; examining very carefully

Going round in circles: seemingly busy but not getting much done

Gold-digger: one woman who uses her beauty to exploit men for their money

Golden oldie: elderly who is still working and old songs that people still enjoy

Golden parachute: "part of an employment contract in which a business person is promised a large amount of money if they [sic] have to leave their [sic] job"

Gyp: overcharging—price gouging

Halo: corona—circle seen around the moon or sun when there is an eclipse

Hang-up: something that one does not want others to know about oneself

Happy hour: a time where some workers stop to socialize and relax in the evenings before going home and prices of beverages and alcohol are reduced at that time

Hatchet man/woman: an employee who is responsible for making changes much to the dismay of co-workers

Have the shakes: trembles greatly, especially out of fear, not illness.

Have your head screwed on: to act sensibly

Heavy: Avoid using the word for adding too much to something—heavy on salt; foot too heavy on the brakes or gas pedal— i.e. putting too much pressure on

Heck/for the heck of it: doing something for enjoyment though that action may be scorned and criticized by others or might even get one in trouble

Help yourself: to take something without permission

Hit a problem; hit trouble: a sudden unfortunate circumstance that occurs

Hit the point dead on; to give the right answer

Hobnob with someone: to try to be in the company of someone important

Hokum: an unrealistic film or play that lacks deep insight

Hole up/be hold up: hiding to save your life as in a bank robbery or in a hurricane

Hold out on somebody: not giving in to that person's demand

Hold your horses: Be patient.

Holistic: like generic medicine, or generalizing about everything without deductive reasoning

Homer: not Homer's *Odyssey*: a baseball player who hits the ball so far away that he/she can run all the bases before the ball gets to a base that he or she has not reached

Hooch: an illegal drink

Hood: neighborhood

Hoodlum: a dissident, one who does not abide by the law

Hook you up: getting a date for someone

Hooker: prostitute, whore

Horny: feels like having sex; wears attire that arouses sexual feelings

Hot on the trail or tracks: Police or citizens will soon catch the culprit.

Howling: should not be used to describe angry attitude or success

Hubby: husband, spouse

Hunk: should not be used to describe a big, sexually attractive, muscular man

Hysterical: Finding someone's problems enjoyable/hysterical is unacceptable—informal

Iffy: a sense of uncertainty; not a good probability

Info: information

In-laws: relatives through spouse's family

Into something or somebody: care about the thing or person; to show much interest in

Intro: introduction

Invite—not "your invite": invitation

In your face: to be too aggressive to others, causing conflict, with bad attitude

Juicy: interesting news, usually gossip; the idea that a particular something will make much money or that that thing coming to fruition will bring happiness

Jiggle: moving all the time, usually from side to side

Jazzy: usually colorful clothing or music with jazz rhythm

Jittery: very nervous

John: toilet (modern usage) or lavatory

Jumping someone: attacking the person by surprise as in a robbery or rape assault

Jumpy: nervous

Jump down someone's throat: to respond harshly to someone who speaks to you with kindness

Jump the light: not stopping when the traffic light is on red.

Keep your cool: controlling one's emotion even when upset

Kinky: different from normal individuals—like a pervert or sadist; may have fetishes

Knockout: attractive, well dressed

Kosher: honest or legal

Know-it-all: one who thinks he or she knows everything, a wiseacre

Laying down the law: making one's wishes clearly known

Lose your cool: easily flustered or angered even over trivial incidents

Loud mouth: usually very cantankerous, quarrelsome, having bad temper

Make an issue out of something: fussing over trivial matters

Mess around: cheat on one's spouse; guilty of infidelity

Mess: Do not use for filth, body excrement—stool (not seat)

Mono: mononucleosis—a fever caused by malfunctioning of certain glands

Nit-picking: very hard to please; expect perfection

Not an issue: something that is insignificant or important, at least, to others

Not on the radar screen: colloquial when used for something not discussed or not widely known

Over the hill: to be old and seemingly unattractive, especially to young people

Pick-me-up: take something like cocaine, marijuana, prescribed drugs, coffee, alcohol to feel rejuvenated

Pitching in: joining a group to help

Poop: same as stool (not seat); filth

Pop the question: to ask someone's hand in marriage

Put in the back of the mind: not thinking about the issue

Put out: give sex to someone, as in the modern trend among "friends with benefit"

Putting someone down: saying unkind things to the person about himself or herself—belittling, ridiculing to hurt the individual

Raise hell: to make a fuss to show that you are annoyed at something or with someone

Raise rumpus: same as raise hell

Rasta: Rastafarian is the correct name for one who does not comb the hair but lets it grow in tangles called dreadlocks or dreads (e.g. Bob Marley). Such person holds the belief that the Ethiopian Emperor Haile Selassie is god and that repatriation to Africa is necessary for Blacks to connect with their ancestral roots.

Red flags: suspected signs of danger

Scare the duke out of me: to frighten someone unexpectedly

Scoop: latest gossip or new

Scream your head off: to laugh relentlessly

Shifty: looks dishonest

Something comes back to haunt: usually bad karma

Son of a bitch: a bad individual with horrible traits and behavior; insensitive to others

Son of a gun: same as son of a bitch

Snitch: to tell somebody's business usually to authority so that person will be in trouble

Snoop around: to be inquisitive; searching people's places without permission

Specs: eye-glasses, glasses, spectacles

Suck it up; Deal with the problem, or do not worry about it.

Sweating small stuff: worrying about trivialities

Smack: hitting someone

That takes the cake: something that merits praise or recognition—extraordinary feat

That's a classic: something that happens but is not surprising, often out of stupidity

To be even: No one owes the other—not necessarily monetary

To be in a jam: to have troubles/problems without any immediate solution

To be on the books: be on the payroll—sometimes illegally

To be on someone's good/bad books: to get favors because one is loved/ not get favors because people do not like that individual

To be willy-nilly: do things without careful planning; making hasty decisions without thinking of the consequences or outcome

To chip-in: collecting or giving money to help someone in need

To click with someone: to have an immediate liking to someone, not necessarily intimate, but platonic

To do something on the fly: to act very quickly, spontaneously

To get a couple of shakes: to buy or pour a few alcoholic drinks

To get some shut-eye: to go to sleep, usually for a short nap

To get the willies: easily frightened

To have a chip on your shoulder: pompous; refusal to be objective when one is at fault or does not want to be reminded of the truth

To have a lot on your plate: to have too much to do within a limited time

To have a roof over your head: to live in a house despite financial hardships

To have issues: always finding something to complain about, usually from pessimists, co-dependent individuals, and attention-seekers

To knock out a person: to hit/slap the person so hard the he or she becomes unconscious

To knock out an animal: to tranquilize the animal to capture it

To take something on the chin: not complaining when asked to do a task one detests

To talk a lot of crap—("a load of crap"): foolish, nonsensical, irrational talk/ideas

To throw the book at someone: to get maximum sentence from the court's ruling

Under your belt: something already done; already achieved

Up to no good: always breaking some rule or getting in trouble

What went down: exactly as the event(s) happened

When the chips are down: going through the most difficult time in one's life

When something clicks: to finally understand, usually from one's own intuition/ insight

Whippersnapper: an annoying, overly confident young person

Wino: one who drinks too much alcohol or alcoholic beverages and is often in a drunken stupor

Wise-crack: a joke

Wise guy: a person who thinks he or she knows everything, yet often errs

Wolfing down the food: eating greedily, gluttonously

Workaholic: one who works relentlessly during waking hours

Work your heart/guts out: making concentrated effort to do well, to succeed

Worked up: usually to become very angry or animated over something

Working against the clock: trying to get things done before the time expected

Working around the clock: staying busy all the time

Work your tail off: working tirelessly; not stopping to relax and unwind for long—(considered a "workaholic")

NOTES

Credits/Works Cited—MLA Example

TO ALL USERS, SPECIFICALLY STUDENTS

I HAVE ACKNOWLEDGED THE sources borrowed in this workbook in a Works Cited format as a reminder of Modern Language Association's (MLA) documentation style, which most English professors expect in research paper. Be warned that "Works Cited" (without the quotation marks) must be placed in the center, instead of Credits. Your professor will discuss other 2009 updates. Be reminded, too, that depending on your core courses, this format may only be applicable to some assignments. If you are not told which discipline to use, do not be afraid to ask. The Chinese proverb holds true:

> He who asks a question is a fool for five minutes;
> he who does not ask remains a fool forever.

CREDITS

Babbie, Earl R. *Society By Agreement: An Introduction to Sociology*. Belmont: Wadsworth Pub., 1977. 4-5. Print.

Bauman, M. Garrett. *Ideas and details: A Guide to College* Writing. 4th ed. Fort Worth: Harcourt, 2001. 40. Print.

Curran, Daniel J., and Claire M. Renzetti. Eds. *Contemporary Society: Problems and Prospects*. Englewood Cliffs: Prentice Hall, 1994. 377-78. Print.

Devine, Robert A., et al. *America: The People and the Dream*. Glenview: Scott Foreman and Co., 1991. Print.

Epstein, Richard L., and Carolyn Kernberger. *The Pocket Guide to Critical Thinking*. Belmont: Thompson Wadsworth, 2006. 247. Print.

Eschholz, Paul, and Alfred Rosa. *Subject and Strategy: A Writer's Reader*. 11th ed. Boston: Bedford/St. Martin's 2008. 78. Print.

Hacker, Diana, and Nancy Somers. *The Bedford Handbook*. 7th ed. Boston: Bedford/St. Martin, 2010. 83. Print.

King, Stephen. "On Writing." *The Conscious Reader*. Ed. Caroline Shrodes et al. 10th ed. Boston: Pearson Education, Inc., 2006. 367. Print.

Loewen, James W. *Lies My Teacher Told Me: Everything Your American History Textbook Got Wrong*. New York: Touchstone—Simon and Schuster, 1996. 170. Print.

Miller, Robert Keith. *Motives for Writing*. 5th ed. New York: McGraw Hill, 2006. 551. Print.

Odell, Lee, Richard Vacca, and Renée Hobbs. *Elements of Language*. Boston: Holt, Rhinehart and Winston, 2001. 941. Print.

Ralph, Phillip Lee. *The Renaissance in Perspective*. New York: St. Martin's P, 1973. 247. Print.

Shrodes, Caroline. et al. *The Conscious Reader*. 10th ed. Boston: Pearson Education, Inc., 2006. 595. Print.

Wehmeirer, Sallly, and Michael Ashby. Ed. *Oxford Advanced Learner's Dictionary*. 6th ed. 2000. Print.

Answer Keys

Note: Since there is no one way to explain or define terminologies, the explanations are only possible ways to revise each. Your explanation, therefore, does not have to be word for word—verbatim—as the ones given. Be sure, nonetheless, to maintain original meanings.

Exercise 1

1. Circle "not the end of the world": replace with inevitable
2. Circle "pretty much pulled the stunts": used all the strategies
3. Circle "threw a fit": became very upset
4. put check; has no cliché
5. Circle "let themselves go" eat gluttonously
6. Circle "hanging out": going regularly
7. Circle "got me pumped up": excited; thrilled
8. Circle "get off your high horse": Be realistic or be less judgmental:
   --"born with a gold spoon in the mouth": not born in affluence or with wealth
9. Circle "pick on": ridicule; target; badger
10. Circle "what buttons to push": weaknesses; foibles; shortfalls
    --"riled up": Revision: upset; irritated; offended; perturbed; vexed

Exercise 2

1. The boys and I show equal interest in fostering an intimate relationship.
2. The committee's decision regarding the proposal was not debatable.
3. Religious controversies will always incite philosophical dogmatism.
4. After sacrificing financially and emotionally for my siblings, their ingratitude is inconceivable.
5. As the pastor addressed the congregation about forgiving those who have wronged us, I thought of a new idea.
6. Correct
7. When I am lonely and bored, to avoid depression, I like to socialize with my friends.

8. James and Suzan study for mathematics examination, so both pass with high grades (or with As).
9. Robert Reich, a social class expert, says, "Social class is a very [controversial] topic."
10. Correct

Exercise 3

1. crazy schedules: disorganized; overloaded; too much to do; overfull
2. a piece of chop liver: feeling helpless; unable to help; can do nothing to solve the problem
3. shoved down their throats: inadequately taught; not well prepared; not enforced; not emphasized enough
4. putting food on the table: not adequately preparing for the family—maybe not having enough food, clothing, a safe home, ability to pay for extra-curricular activities, no savings for children's college education
5. X
6. a new lease on life: not their destiny or fate; a second chance to live;
7. twenty-four seven: norm; day-to-day habit; routine; customary pattern; daily
8. flipped out: became upset; lost his temper; was furious, livid, irate, or other synonym
9. X
10. going solo: going alone

Exercise 4

Possible Revisions. Replace underlined section with revised phrase
1. America needs to <u>jump on the bandwagon</u> to clean up the environment to control global warming and to be more competitive with China in education and productivity NV revised: needs to support the team of environmentalists or to participate in the effort
2. Having a balanced diet, getting adequate sleep, and doing regular exercise promote good health.
   *Draw / through the number 2
3. "Foolish" is often a stigma assigned to young people, but many prove that they <u>have a good head on their shoulder.</u> NV
   * Revised: ... they are intelligent, sensible, mature, conscientious, show a sense of responsibility, or similar synonym
4. Most addicts do not want help until they <u>hit rock bottom.</u> NV

*Revised: … until they cannot function normally, rationally; until they lose physical and emotional stability; until their health is severely affected

5. The exercise challenge is so difficult that the obese participants <u>quit cold turkey</u>. NV

   Revised: give up; refuse to try; accept defeat; cannot be bothered; stop exercising

6. If these negative individuals refuse to change, we should <u>kick them to the curb</u>. NV

   *Revised: dissociate ourselves; avoid them; ask them to leave the group

7. It is stereotypically believed that many Asian-Americans chose in vitro fertilization to have boys over girls. (see number 2)

8. The former Illinois Governor Blagovojevich is very <u>mad</u> at Congress who impeached him for his alleged effort to sell President Obama's senate seat. NV

   * Revised: upset; displeased; angry at the group—the institution as a whole/with individuals, or similar synonymous phrases

9. Sarah Palin, former governor of Alaska, has a <u>grouse</u> against the media for treating her unfairly because she is a woman. NV

   *Revised: complaint; grievance

10. When the President of the United States vetoes a bill, he disagrees with the proposal(s). (as in number 2)

Exercise 5

Possible Phrasings

1. do something to inhibit that person's success; create opposition
2. thick skin—be able to take constructive criticism; thin skin—(inability to accept any form of criticism, extremely sensitive, gets upset easily
3. something that is quite baffling; to be in awe of something or somebody
4. continually dancing—almost incessantly showing off dancing skills
5. to cope with a problem or find a solution without being overly flustered
6. having much to do within a short time
7. a family that has a good relationship; friends who get along without much fussing and fighting—(both groups have very little disagreements)
8. being too close to someone's face especially when arguing
9. cannot foresee any immediate or possible solution to an important problem/issue
10. inability to respond spontaneously when asked a question

Exercise 6

Essay may be assigned. CS =comma splice
1. CS between world and since
2. CS between died and in addition
3. CS between embryos and as of

Exercise 7

See Comma splice at underlined areas.

Sometimes when we argue, it's easy to get carried away. Remember that your goal is to persuade and perhaps change your readers, not alienate <u>them, instead</u> of laying on insults or sarcasm, present your ideas in a moderate let-us-reason-together spirit. Such a tone will persuade your readers that you are sincere in your attempts to argue as truthfully and fairly as <u>possible, if</u> your readers do not respect you as a reasonable person, they certainly won't be swayed to your side of an issue. Don't preach or pontificate either; no one likes—or respects—a writer with a superior <u>attitude, write</u> in your natural "voice"; don't adopt a pseudo-intellectual tone. In short, to argue effectively, you should sound logical, sincere, and informed.

Exercise 8

Comma splices underlined

The Renaissance was a testing time for beliefs that had been held, sometimes very feebly, for many centuries. It was also a period when new ideas and forces were beginning to come into play. Hence the Renaissance was both modern and medieval—as is, for that matter, the "modern" age, which exhibits some emotional attitudes and beliefs that go back to medieval, ancient, even prehistoric <u>times, the</u> Renaissance material base was a late medieval heritage—urban populations, a money economy, and the beginning of a capitalist enterprise, with small but thriving cities to foster and disseminate culture. These socio-economic factors, so essential to the whole modern era, were not originated by or in the Renaissance. In fact, to some extent they were temporarily impaired during the fourteenth and fifteenth centuries by a drastic decline in population following the Black Death and by a contraction of industry and commerce in Italy and portions of northern Europe, accompanied by severe financial crisis. If modern society is dependent on the prominence of a middle class—the origins of which can be traced to the late Middle Ages—the trend in the leading centers of Italian Renaissance civilization was <u>retrogressive, between</u> the thirteenth and the late fifteenth centuries[,] the urban middle class in Italy—the most advanced region of European civilization—shrank in numbers and influence as commercial oligarchies gained ascendancy. Italian society was more aristocratic in tone at the end of the Renaissance than at the beginning, and in Europe as a whole the democratic tendencies implicit in the growth of self-governing towns during the late Middle Ages—in France, the Netherlands, and Germany as well as Italy—had been largely suppressed, it is true that some important changes in interests and activities pointed in a modern direction, notably increased travel, the introduction of printed books, and fumbling but essential efforts to unlock the secrets of nature. But it is [also] true that other equally important aspects of Renaissance society and culture were still oriented towards the past.

Exercise 9

Write short paragraph.
  1. Comma splice between <u>time</u> and the <u>figure</u>

Exercise 10

Essay may also be required.
  1. comma splice between **them** and a **decent** (par. 1)
  2. comma splice between it is their right and it is their duty (par 2)
     *Notice how modern sentence structures and punctuation rules are dissimilar from the archaic style Jefferson's era. Note how the punctuation rules are broken and the fragmented sentences.

Exercise 11

One and a half page narrative needed.
  1. *Reason being that I can take all that I have learned and apply it to real life
  2. Human cloning, a scientific phenomenon, has sparked controversial debates among scientists, moralists, and Christians, so much so that government has vetoed any possibility of creating a human being.
  3. *Is the fact that the economic recession affects even the wealthy.
  4. The racial divide in America is narrowing, but there are still milestones to go to bridge the educational, economic, and political gap.
  5. *In the mean time, coping with the stress of going to college, being a full-time mother, and working full time
  6. *Which is not to imply that developed countries are not plagued with social problems such as poverty and unemployment.

7. *Being an independent person who makes conscientious decisions to ensure the success of her children.

Exercise 12

Added writing is expected
1. Two (2) fragments (see underline)

The coming of the first Americans took place long before the writing of history began. How then do archeologists piece together the story of their arrival? The major way is by studying ancient **artifacts**—objects made by human beings. <u>By examining such things as stone arrowheads, bone tools, or pieces of fur clothing.</u> Archeologists can make reason-able guesses about how early peoples may have lived.

To locate artifacts, archeologists search for places where early people might have camped or hunted. <u>Because thousands of years separate us from the first Americans,</u> many objects have been covered up or destroyed. Therefore, archeologists often must sift carefully through many layers of soil … [in a] … place … called an archeological dig.

—Devine et al., "The First Americans"

Exercise 13

Most readers feel comfortable reading paragraphs that range between one hundred and two hundred words. Shorter paragraphs force too much stopping and starting, and longer ones strain readers' attention span. There are exceptions to this guideline, however. Paragraphs longer than two hundred words frequently appear in scholarly <u>writing where they suggest seriousness and depth</u>. Paragraphs shorter than one hundred words occur in newspaper because of narrow <u>columns, in</u> informal essays to quicken the pace, and in business writing and Web <u>sites where</u> readers routinely skim for main ideas.

In an essay, the first and last paragraphs will ordinarily be the conclusion. These special-purpose paragraphs are likely to be shorter than [those] in the body of the essay. Typically, the body paragraph will follow the essay's outline: one paragraph per point in longer essays. Some ideas require more development than <u>others,</u> … so it is best to be flexible. If an idea stretches to a length unreasonable for a <u>paragraph, you</u> should divide the <u>paragraph, even</u> if you have presented comparable points … in single paragraphs.

Exercise 14

Underlined sections show where errors should be corrected.

A creative thinker must peek behind unquestioned ideas once in a while to keep from being close-minded. Doing this has led to some of humankind's most creative concepts. The Declaration of Independence challenged the divine right of kings—the unquestioned belief that a king received his right to rule from God. Thomas Jefferson questioned this by stating that "All men are created equal" and that a king should rule, not by God's authority, but by "the consent of the governed." What changes so few words have made in the world!

For centuries the dissection of the human body was forbidden. Until this unquestioned idea was challenged and the body dissected, people believed our emotions came from our our hearts (not our minds) and even thought a man's erection came from air in his lungs.

Unquestioned ideas are invisible to us because almost everyone takes them for granted, like eyesight or the ability to walk. When I mentioned Thomas Jefferson's famous phrases, did you go one step further and ask if "all men are created equal," and [if] "consent of the governed" [is] also [being questioned] today? If challenging these ideas is upsetting, it's because our belief in them is deeply ingrained. [Buddha also reminds us to "Believe nothing because a belief is generally held"].

Exercise 15

Underlined areas show fragments and where they should be connected.

On rare occasions, individuals with neither vast armies nor vast congregations have succeeded in exerting influence well beyond national boundaries. Like the successful leaders of nations that we've already examined, they have done so because of the persuasiveness of their stories and the steadfastness with which they have reinforced those stories through their manner of living. In the twentieth century, three men stand out as exemplars in this category: Mohandas (Mahatma) Gandhi, Nelson Mandela, and Jean Monnet.

Perhaps the most well-known is Gandhi. Growing up in undistinguished surroundings in the late nineteenth-century colonial India, Gandhi spent time in England as a young man and then lived for twenty years in South Africa. There he was horrified by the mis-treatment by European colonizers of Indians and other "persons": he read widely in philosophy and religion; ... he became involved in various protests. Returning to his native India at the start of the World War 1, Gandhi perfected methods of satyagraha—peaceful (non-violent) protest (or resistance). Alongside devoted countrymen, [he] led series of strikes and protest marches, destined to throw into sharp relief the difference between the brutal English masters—who sought to hold power at any cost—and the non-belligerent Indians. These protests were choreographed to underscore the nobility of the native cause and the reasonableness with which Indians were striving to express their goals. Gandhi's overt message was: "We do not seek to make war or shed blood. We only want to be treated as fellow human beings. Once we have achieved the status of equals, we have no further claims."

In one sense, Gandhi's message could not have been simpler: It can be traced back to Christ and to the other religious leaders. Yet, it also clashed with an entrenched counter-story: that one can only attain an equal status vis-à-vis one's colonizers if—like the United States in the late eighteenth century or South America in the early nineteenth century—one is willing to go to war. Moreover, Gandhi did not only have a simple linguistic message; he also developed an integrated program of prayer, fasting, and facing one's opponent without weapons, even willing to do so until death. His embodiment of the message could not have been more dramatic; it went well beyond verbal expression, to include a whole range of evocative formats, such as his squatting on the ground and operating a simple machine for spinning cloth.

Gandhi's story reverberated around the world. While annoying some (Churchill memorably disparaged him as that "Half-naked fakir"), it inspired many leaders and ordinary citizens—ranging from Martin Luther King Jr. in the American South in the early 1960s, to the students who rallied for greater democracy in Tiananmen Square in Beijing in 1989.

Like Gandhi, Nelson Mandela embodied a message that resonated on a level far beyond the borders of … South Africa. Indeed, of all the leaders in recent years, Mandela is widely considered one of the most impressive and influential. A lawyer by training, [he] became actively involved in resistance as part of the African National Congress. At first, he embraced non-violent resistance, but after a series of frustrating and degrading encounters, he joined a paramilitary group. Narrowly escaping death by combat or judicial sentence, [he] was imprisoned for twenty-seven years. Although such an experience would likely have demoralized, radicalized, or marginalized most other persons—especially since it occurred at middle age, often considered the apogee of an individual's person power—imprisonment seemed only to fortify Mandela.

Rather than seeking revenge against his opponents and jailers, Mandela called for re-conciliation. He was convinced—and was able to convince others—that South Africa could not function as a society unless it could put its wrenching history behind it. Under the leadership of Nobel Peace Prize Winner Archbishop Desmond Tuto, Mandela convened a Commission of Truth and Reconciliation. The Gandhian idea behind this commission was that it would seek to establish what actually happened during the years of apartheid but would not attempt to sit in ultimate judgment. The truth having been established as well as it could be, citizens of varying persuasions could come to terms with the past and commit their future energies to the buildup of a new and more fully re-presentative society. <u>A master of non-verbal as well as verbal</u> <u>forms, Mandela</u> asked his one time jailer to sit in the front row during his presidential inaugural ceremony.

Mandela succeeded in changing the minds not only of millions of his otherwise diverse fellow citizens but equally of millions of observers around the world—few of whom would have predicted that South Africa [would] become a new nation without decades of bloodshed. Ideas like Commission on Truth and Reconciliation have traveled across national boundaries. The tipping points for Mandela's success entail both his exemplary behavior after his release from jail and the willingness of the entrenched South African leadership to negotiate with him—both examples reflecting [his] personal resonance, among other things.

A third figure of global importance worked largely behind the scenes: the French economist and diplomat Jean Monnet, born in 1888. When his comfortable life was shattered by the events of World War 1, Monnet—a careful and reflective student of his-tory—pondered why it was necessary for European countries to go to war, as they had intermittently since the time of Charlemagne more than a thousand years before. He began to work towards the creation of institutions, that could bring about a united Europe. After the trauma of world War 1, the collapse of the League of Nations, the rise of fascism, and the unprecedented warfare of World War 11, a lesser person would have concluded that attempts to build a European community were futile. Monnet was a firm believer in his own oft-repeated slogan: "I regard every defeat (or challenge) as an opportunity. <u>Amid the physical and psychological ruins of</u> <u>war-torn Europe, Monnet</u> envisioned—and proceeded to sow—the seeds of a larger European polity.

Exercise 16

1. No
2. Yes. Nowadays, deoxyribonucleic acid (DNA) tests provide proof to force negligent fathers, who deny the existence of their children, to accept <u>responsibility. If</u> they refuse, the courts will enforce the law by stipulating rigid fines or imprisonment.
3. Yes. Liberal arts program ensures that all college graduates are exposed to a wide array of <u>knowledge. This</u> allows even those from the most impoverished socio-economic backgrounds and communities to become well-rounded and academically cultured.
4. No.

5. Yes. Learning is a continuous process, consciously and <u>subconsciously. Many</u>, however, seem to relish in the bliss of ignorance and denial about the value of education.
6. No.
7. Yes. Any good government must ensure adequate funding in the budget for advanced <u>education. This</u> ensures that young people will have the opportunity to get advanced training to fill positions that demand academic knowledge and specialized skills.

Exercise 17

It is scientifically proven that human beings are intrinsically social creatures and that socialization is pertinent to <u>survival. Their</u> finding is substantiated by numerous studies done my sociologists, anthropologists, archeologists, psychologists, and others schools of thought who further contend that one only has to observe nature itself to understand human interaction in correlation with the eco-<u>system. It</u> is evident that all creatures function within certain boundaries and within in-groups. Watch various birds in the air and on land, the schools of fish in the wide expanse of the oceans, seas, and rivers, the beasts of the fields, human beings at large in their ethnic groups versus in diverse gatherings, and even the variations of plants within certain climatic <u>regions. It</u> seems that, except for the recluse, who consciously decides to exclude himself or herself from the human chain to live in a vacuum, all other living things operate within the confines of their in-groups: family, friends, organizations, associations, <u>institutions. This</u> socialization process becomes an integral part of human need not only to fulfill Abraham Maslov's hierarchy of needs—provision of food, shelter, and clothing—but also the need to feel part of a group, to develop self-actualization within the boundaries of those groups. While some prey on others, and the strong sometimes oppress the weak in organized societies and local communities, there is a universal understanding that every individual is innately gifted to serve a particular purpose in shaping the bond of humanity which is a clear indication that "No man [or woman] is an island."

Exercise 18

You have ten minutes to complete this exercise (in-class warm-up exercise)

I also want to speak to the Muslims throughout the <u>world. We</u> respect your <u>faith.</u> <u>It</u> is practiced freely by many Americans and by millions more in countries that America counts as <u>friends. Its</u> teachings are good and peaceful, and those who commit evil in the name of Allah blaspheme the name of Allah. The terrorists are traitors to their own faith, trying, in effect, to hijack Islam itself. The enemy of America is not our many Muslim friends; it is not our many Arab friends. Our enemy is the radical network of terrorists and every government the supports them.

Our war on terror begins with Al Quaeda, but it does not end <u>there. It</u> will not end until every terrorist group of the global reach has been formed, stopped and defeated. Americans are asking, "Why do they hate us?"

Exercise 19

1. today and according.
2. thirty and one
3. Present and it

Exercise 20

Expository Essay

Exercise 21

1. Underline, then put period between <u>group</u> and <u>it is</u> (run-on or fused sentence)
2. <u>Because it is commonly understood</u> (frag.—fragment)
3. Underline: People <u>are expected</u> (t—faulty tense).
4. Underline <u>Textbook … illustrate</u> (vb.—subject-verb agreement)
5. Underline <u>wrong language</u> and <u>it means</u> (comma splice)
6. Sentences without error: --People **to** clearly
                                        --In the U.S. **to** speech
                                        --It is used **to** know well
                                      --It is the language **to** government
                                      --It is also the variety **to** grammar books
                                      --Nobody **to** necessary

Exercise 22

1. For years, as the costs of medical care have soared (fragment)
2. physicians have grown (grammar: subject-verb disagreement)
3. Put period between patient and as a result (run-on or fused sentence).
4. people don't or more formal "do not" (subject-verb disagreement)
5. Put period between insurance company and this naturally (comma splice)

Exercise 23

1. Humanity's independence seems, not seem ...
2. Put period (full stop BrE) between Qur'an and we.
3. Put period (.) or semicolon (;), preferably period between machines and the unskilled.
4. Replace the period after "organized society" with a colon (:) and lower the capital "I" in Institution, **to link the fragmented list**.

Exercise 24

1. an agreement can be defined
2. We create, not we creates.
3. Agreements and disagreements do not reflect, **not** does not ... reflects **(subjects joined by and need plural verb)**
4. agreements have, not agreements **has**
5. never met (in this sentence structure) not **never meet**
6. You share, not shares.
7. You may **have argued**, not **have argue**.

Exercise 25

1. <u>Everybody</u> has a right to <u>his or her</u> opinion (their is plural; everybody is singular)
2. The reason the three new employees lose the job is their lackadaisical attitude and repetitive tardiness (reason why; reason is because are both redundant)
3. If a country cannot sustain itself, there is not much hope for the future generation, especially children who are orphaned at an early age (add a subject to the fragment).
4. A positive approach to life can be achieved through spirituality, but there are skeptics, agnostics, and others who believe otherwise (comma splice between spirituality and there).
5. Joan protests, "I have no money" (cliché: break the bank).
6. My friends and I appreciate the kind gesture of the financial and emotional support received (Never put self first in formal writing; subjects joined by and take plural verb).
7. no error

Exercise 26

1. C
2. During peer editing, writers will get a number of suggestions that they may not appreciate but should always examine the relevance of the commentary to improve writing skills.
3. Some students are offended by professors' grades because they are unaware of the fundamental rules of English thus often write the way they speak on a day-to-day basis.
4. C
5. Students seldom see the errors in their essays, as they might not spend enough time editing, or they might not know what is wrong, or they might not know how to correct repetitive mistakes.

Exercise 27

1. X If <u>one</u> wants to achieve success, <u>one</u> must start making sensible choices at an early age.
2. Put a check
3. Put a check
4. Put a check
5. X If global warming continues at its present rate, it will cause drastic changes in the ozone layers which climatologists contend will eventually create more severe temperature variation on earth, causing landforms to develop fault lines

Exercise 28

1. It is important for a parent to intervene before or when his or her child—young or old—becomes addicted to any drug, especially cocaine, heroin, and marijuana.
2. Neither James nor his friends are … army training.
3. In America, everyone who is arrested should be read the Miranda Rights.
4. To survive in a changing economy and in the age of technological advancement, one must be flexible in accepting changes if one does not want to be stagnant in personal growth.
5. Do nothing.

Exercise 29

1. Constitutionally, human beings are entitled to free speech, "life, liberty, and the pursuit of happiness," but they must be aware that every privilege comes with limitations.
2. Patriotic citizens often support any movement or change that uplifts their country or community.
3. no change
4. In Florida, as in most states, a seventeen year-old minors who commit a crime can and may be treated as adults in the courts, depending on the crime they commit.
5. no change

Exercise 30

Possible Revisions
1. The surgeon elaborates, "Everyone [is] watching the chin protrude with the injected serum and [is noticing] how easy the process is."
2. When Jill began to look through the table of contents, she realized the book had no information for her research paper
3. The home owner's association charged the new residents an exorbitant fee of $550 per month for maintenance fee and justified the cost to the recent upgrades in particular residences
5. Correct

Exercise 31

Possible Revisions
1. Students/learners/writers who wish to get A in writing must be competent in the overall mechanics.
2. A member may become the target of his or her own gang by disagreeing with the group's ideologies or by breaking the code of conduct.
3. If instructions are not read before carrying out a proven process, there is the tendency to make mistakes by using "trial and error.'
4. When people do not work hard, they limit their capabilities.
5. A given task should be done to the best of one's ability.

Exercise 32

Possible Revisions

1. Young people/Youths/Younger adults can avoid many mistakes if they follow the wisdom of the elders
2. More often than not, especially the among the educated, those who believe in necrophilia, necromancy, and voodoo will be ridiculed.
3. Most psychologists suggest finding one's own path to happiness.
4. Taking deep breaths at intervals is one suggestion to combat a heart attack
5. Parents do not know if their children will succeed or not, as the choices made will determine that.

Exercise 33

Possible Revisions:

1. Medical researchers/farmers/distributors/scientists/food handlers. are unsure whether it is the tomato or other vegetables that is causing the widespread salmonella poisoning in a number of states.
2. Revising the age-old curriculum/universal health care/remodeling the classrooms is not is not the committee's priority.
3. If the athletes/swimmers/tennis players, they will have to put in one hundred hours of practice.
4. The in-coming interns/volunteers/ may be unaware that scientists usually test theories by conducting experiments repeatedly
5. Procrastination/Ignoring post-secondary education/Not reading avidly is a bad idea.

Exercise 34

Possible Revisions

1. Those who want to achieve greatness have to work hard and be prudent.
2. Volunteering at the homeless shelter is good way to serve in the community.
3. Nature lovers often observe animals' behavior in their natural habitat then write books to share their findings
4. Doctors concur that too much carbohydrates and sugary foods endanger the health of patients with diabetes 2.
5. Socrates, Buddha, and other renowned philosophers of all centuries encourage everyone to analyze all ideologies passed down as traditions as well as new notions.

Exercise 35

Descriptive essay (no you or your if possible)

Exercise 36

Individual work with FANBOYS: coordinating conjunctions (for, and, nor, but, or, yet, so)

Exercise 37

1. life; however,
2. Despite the expense,
3. Notwithstanding,
4. Thoreau, for example,
5. perseverance, nonetheless,

Exercise 38

1. In fact,
2. media, for example,
3. For instance,
4. parent, in disguise,
5. Furthermore,
6. As a result,
7. Many, nonetheless,
8. On the other hand,

Exercise 39

Comparison and Contrast essay: Your professor will decide the length and may also change the time given.

Exercise 40

Possible Revisions
1. Delete: Let me tell you something
   --I emphasize: No child should be sexually abused.
2. Delete: "can" and "just fine" (possible replacements—well; intelligently; clearly)
   -- I write well.

3. Delete: from the get go (slang)
   --Though the witnesses swore on the Bible that they saw the heist, it was not true.
4. Delete: I could not believe my eyes (too wordy and trite for college writing)
   I was shocked when I saw an alligator of that enormity basking in sun near the lake in front of my apartment.
5. Find a synonym or a more collegiate phrase (e.g. instantly; in an instant) for "the next thing you know."
   --In an instant, the driver swerves then hits the guard wall
6. Delete: so you can see
   --Health insurance should be one of every tax payer's constitutional rights.
7. "In fact," is an adequate introductory phrase. The added verbiage makes the phrasing too wordy. Note comma placement, also.
8. Delete: relieve stress on mother Earth
   --To protect the earth's formation, cutting down forests must be curtailed
9. Delete years down the road (not needed)
   --Climatologists predict that global warming will cause glaciers to melt causing Florida and New York City to be flooded like New Orleans
10. Delete: As I was saying (no addition needed)
    --Sales of houses have declined in many states since 2007.

Exercise 41

1. I am writing to tell you
2. way out of proportion
3. In my opinion
4. Do nothing.
5. I guess you can say
6. believe it or not
7. back in the day
8. "walk the walk and talk the talk" ; cool; lame
9. sat Jean down
10. I would like to say

Exercise 42

Your own explanation is needed for any changes made, and the professor may discuss your explanations as a whole-class exercise.

1. For my conclusion; I want you to believe me; took the life out of me
2. No change
3. What was killing me then and is still killing me now …
4. went through hell and high water
5. the name of the game
6. Right then and there
7. tumbling over the place
8. No change
9. Before I knew it
10. As of now

Exercise 43

1. kind of; cute
2. partied … away
3. in the heat of the moment
4. in my life
5. get the best of him
6. honestly speaking
7. sort of
8. starting to come around
9. you bet
10. lo and behold

Exercise 44

1. The direction to Niagara Falls is on the sign ahead.
2. She accepted the job being aware of the danger of espionage.
3. Traveling and internships allow one to gain experience.
4. Ida explains that she does not want to be ruthless and insensitive.
5. When Jane learns of her friends' disloyalty, she disassociates herself from the group.
6. When the burglars broke into our house, my heart palpitated greatly.
7. Men in my neighborhood call me a snob because I am ambitious
8. Circle the number.
9. After the shots were fired, Paul exclaimed, "I am going to die!"
10. The bullies' arrests were overdue, as they were too fierce and forward

CPSIA information can be obtained
at www.ICGtesting.com
Printed in the USA
LVHW060257080921
697290LV00012B/608